Francis J. Morley M. D.

Pulitzer Prize Poems

PULITZER PRIZE

Poems

COMPILED BY MARJORIE BARROWS

RANDOM HOUSE · NEW YORK

41 - 5,888

To

GRACE HAMMILL

PUBLISHER'S FOREWORD

HERE IS a much needed book that presents some of the best poems that, during the past two decades, have been written in America.

The books from which these poems have been chosen have won the highest award given to American poets—the Pulitzer Prize. The poems which have been selected are not the highly difficult poems appreciated by the few, but the simpler, better-loved poems that a larger American public has already greeted with enthusiasm.

This first collection from the work of all the Pulitzer Prize poets should find a welcome from poetry readers everywhere, for the richness and beauty of many of these poems make them an enduring addition to our country's literature.

CONTENTS

[ix]

[x]

ACKNOWLEDGMENTS

THE COMPILER wishes to thank the various publishers and agents who have granted permission for the reprinting of the following poems in this book:

"Music I Heard" and "Atlantis," from *Selected Poems*, and "The Day Ended," from *The Pilgrimage of Festus*, by Conrad Aiken, reprinted by permission of Charles Scribner's Sons, publishers.

"Sunderland Capture," "Surf," and "Color Line," from *Sunderland Capture*, by Leonard Bacon, reprinted by permission of Harper & Brothers, publishers.

"Invocation," "The Years Ride Out," "Jubili, Jubilo!" and "John Brown's Body Lies A-Mouldering in the Grave," from *John Brown's Body*, by Stephen Vincent Benét, reprinted by permission of Doubleday, Doran and Company, publishers.

"Eyes Are Lit Up," "A Boy, a Lake, a Sun," "Country Church," "Strange Holiness," "Fireflies in a Graveyard," and "The Pines," from *Strange Holiness*, by Robert P. Tristram Coffin, reprinted by permission of The Macmillan Company, publishers.

"The Dead Elm on the Hilltop," "Memory of Lake Superior," and "The Noise of Leaves," from *The Flowering Stone*, by George Dillon, copyright, 1931,

[xiii]

[xiv]

PULITZER PRIZE AWARDS

*For the best volume of verse published during
the year by an American author*

For 1922   Edwin Arlington Robinson, *Collected Poems*
            (The Macmillan Company)
For 1923   Edna St. Vincent Millay, *The Harp-Weaver*
            (Harper and Brothers) and *A Few Figs
            from Thistles* (Harper and Brothers)
For 1924   Robert Frost, *New Hampshire* (Henry Holt
            and Company)
For 1925   Edwin Arlington Robinson, *The Man Who
            Died Twice* (The Macmillan Company)
For 1926   Amy Lowell, *What's O'Clock* (Houghton
            Mifflin Company)
For 1927   Leonora Speyer, *Fiddler's Farewell* (Alfred
            A. Knopf)
For 1928   Edwin Arlington Robinson, *Tristram* (The
            Macmillan Company)
For 1929   Stephen Vincent Benét, *John Brown's Body*
            (Doubleday, Doran and Company)
For 1930   Conrad Aiken, *Selected Poems* (Charles
            Scribner's Sons)
For 1931   Robert Frost, *Collected Poems* (Henry Holt
            and Company)
For 1932   George Dillon, *The Flowering Stone* (The
            Viking Press)

For 1933   Archibald MacLeish, *Conquistador* (Houghton Mifflin Company)

For 1934   Robert Hillyer, *Collected Verse* (Alfred A. Knopf)

For 1935   Audrey Wurdemann, *Bright Ambush* (The John Day Company)

For 1936   Robert P. Tristram Coffin, *Strange Holiness* (The Macmillan Company)

For 1937   Robert Frost, *A Further Range* (Henry Holt and Company)

For 1938   Marya Zaturenska, *Cold Morning Sky* (The Macmillan Company)

For 1939   John Gould Fletcher, *Selected Poems* (Farrar and Rinehart, Inc.)

For 1940   Mark Van Doren, *Collected Poems* (Henry Holt and Company)

For 1941   Leonard Bacon, *Sunderland Capture* (Harper and Brothers)

Conrad Aiken

MUSIC I HEARD

Music I heard with you was more than music,
And bread I broke with you was more than
        bread;
Now that I am without you, all is desolate;
All that was once so beautiful is dead.

Your hands once touched this table and this
        silver,
And I have seen your fingers hold this glass.
These things do not remember you, beloved,—
And yet your touch upon them will not pass.

For it was in my heart you moved among them,
And blessed them with your hands and with your
        eyes;
And in my heart they will remember always,—
They knew you once, O beautiful and wise.

ATLANTIS

There was an island in the sea
That out of immortal chaos reared
Towers of topaz, trees of pearl
For maidens adored and warriors feared.

Long ago it sunk in the sea;
And now, a thousand fathoms deep,
Sea-worms above it whirl their lamps,
Crabs on the pale mosaic creep.

Voyagers over that haunted sea
Hear from the waters under the keel
A sound that is not wave or foam;
Nor do they only hear, but feel

The timbers quiver, as eerily comes
Up from the dark an elfin singing
Of voices happy as none can be,
And bells an ethereal anthem ringing.

Thereafter, where they go or come,
They will be silent; they have heard
Out of the infinite of the soul
An incommunicable word;

Thereafter, they are as lovers who
Over an infinite brightness lean:
"It is Atlantis!" all their speech;
"To lost Atlantis have we been."

THE DAY ENDED

From The Pilgrimage of Festus

The day ended, and the slow-wheeling magnif-
    icent constellations
Glided like lights of ships down the river of space,
And Festus was disturbed once more, and wished
    to speak,
And heavily raised his head at last in sorrow,
And turned toward the stars his face,
And said: "Look, Festus, how yet once more the
    immortals
Kindle their delicate lanterns and walk in the sky
While you on a lonely hill sit alone in sadness
And remember that you must die!
Look at the stars, Festus, treader of kingdoms,
You who carried the world like a bird in a cage,
You whose heart is a desert, gaunt with winter,
You whose sword in youth was a sevenfold light-
    ning
Now worn and green with age!
Look! the immortals once more in the sky of your
    heart,
The immortals you scorned and forgot,
Walk in the dim blue gardens softly apart
To a music you taught them not! . . ."

[6]

Leonard Bacon

The swallowtail butterfly, over black moving
    marble
Of the pool, swooped down so you could hear the
    flick
Of his wings on the water, bright dipsomaniac,
Sunborn and yellow and thirsty as the sun.
With the sound of a secret kiss he plunged again,
And yet again, and lay with bright wings flat
In sweet and golden exhaustion, floating with the
    stream,
Then, revived, rose up anew into his world
Of air and danger and light. He vanished between
The trunks of trees that were there before I saw
    him,
And will be after both of us have gone,
Inconstant, whether man or butterfly.
But his mad drinking made me thirst for the
    river—
Dark, known, undeciphered, however known—
More even than is my wont. Gone the desire
To take the trout, whose circle gave the pool
Hidden purpose. I was getting with the butterfly
Where I desired to be, by being there.
Tomorrow, I thought, I will fish the Sunderland.

[9]

The Sunderland's unobtrusive, a strip of stream
You would hardly look at from a Pullman
window.
But you never will, thank God! The Sunderland
Can be looked at only, so to say, from within
Its enigmatic alternation of pools
And rapids in their haste, 'mid oak and cat-briar,
Green, flexible, and harsh, laurel like combers
Hanging ere they break, later azalea dropping
Like a veil that hides the secret gods withdrawn,
That dwell in the dark of the mind, known but
not named.
Also there is mud enough, false tongues of swamp,
Where you thought it was all hard gravel or solid
sand.
You rouse black duck and partridge, and in the
windfalls
There is always a dry rustle mocking the liquid
Perpetual music of little cataracts.

It was hot when I got to the stream. And my
mind was hot,
As minds too often are, when small, unsolved
But desperate quandaries run like frightened
beasts
In narrowing circles. Minds are a lot alike
Though we invest the notable ones with powers
And noble exceptions. We think of Einstein as
calm,

Happy, equal to his problem. No doubt he is,
If you limit the problem. But the whole Einstein
        has
Relatively as hard a time with his whole problem
As you with yours. And it's probably as banale,
And you wouldn't understand it, if he dared state
        it,
Any more than you can understand your own,
Which you never could. Nor will you be able to.

My God, it was hot. The jet-winged darning-
        needles,
With bodies like emerald bars, lanced in the light,
And a film of pollen lay on the still backwaters,
Like desert dust on a dead Arab's eye.
Yet cool breathed from the river as I stepped in
And moved downstream, letting my line loop out.
Speech the wise say is always a sort of action.
Action may be a sort of speech. I was speaking
With the rod, because I had no language to utter
The unformed thing that moved in the mind. It
        was there,
Had been for months. I had had glimpses of it,
Had shrunk from it, partly ignorance partly fear,
Had ignored it over a job, forgotten it
At a cocktail party. But now, drifting down-
        stream,
I answered it with ritual discipline
Of the split bamboo. What is that childish spirit

Dwelling on the surface of things, that heals the
     inner
By mere equipping and accouterment,
Putting on the appropriate armor, wearing the
     costume
Of the part, however one may laugh at the part?
There's a strange help in being point device
For a little problem that is pointless enough,
No more than a striking trout by the fallen elm.
Why should that bulk so large in the brighter
     courts
Of a mind that knows gross darkness that can be
     felt?
I cannot answer, save that mechanical
Rhythm of casting has a healing in it,
Or had for me then, as the line undulated
Over a swirl well known. They were striking
     short,
A roiling flash, a stroke that bent the tip,
And something lost, as the image of a dream
Is lost in the bright morning. Lost or not,
I hardly cared, because the water and shadow
Were taking possession. The layer of feeling I
     moved in
Extended itself into a lonely world,
Of which I was in my way the lonely maker,
Who found his work good. Violets and herb-
     robert
Were doubtless there before I came downstream.

But whence came the proprietary creative
Sense of them, that was more and less than
        thought,
In spite of the invincible I was escaping,
Fleeing from, if you like? One must retreat
When one is ambushed by the undefined.
Later we may define it. So hope flatters.
But mere possessive darkness of the pools
Was drawing me away from hope and fear,
As if they mattered. And what if one drew blank
Even here in little? One draws blank in the large,
And may ignore it, if one will but learn
This art of drifting, drifting—disembodied,
Or better liberated from the tyrannic
Repetition of the unwisdom of the mind.

There is a long reach on the Sunderland,
One of those places where, when you come there
        first,
Two things are mixed in your thoughts. It has a
        strangeness
It never has lost for me. And yet I had known it
Always, before I knew it, as if innate.
It is shaped as a mind would shape a river, if
A mind shaped rivers. Between phalanxes
Of the red willow the stream is the clear thought
Of water, but beneath the maple glooms
At the end of the stretch it has turned deep and
        gray

As a phoebe's crest, yet has the mineral gleam
Of the darker striping in onyx. I lashed the fly
In under the overhang with a listless flick,
The gesture of one who says: Shoot and be
    damned!
For the gust of the art was failing, and I was tired
Of the heat, the glare, the silence.
Nevertheless the cast was good. It went
Bullet-like to the swirling target. The eddy took
The fly deep down in its stone-colored bosom
Under the maple bough. How should I have
    known
The attending fury that split time in two
When it hit the hackle, how all life and fire
Would come in color and calamity
To a world redressed by drive and anger, refusal
Of any defeat? Or know that minim resistance
Was akin to the nebula's that hurls away
From the pull of a train of stars?

        In the woods that evening
The flag-flowers stood. Their purple from the
    dusk
Borrowed a darker glory than day lends them.
Shadow made color substance that the mind,
Hovering, dipped down to and drank like the
    butterfly,
While in the swirl and eddy under thought
Wildness swam gleaming.

SURF

It's a long three miles to the curved white shore,
Yet the woods grow wondrous with the roar.
Through silver-belted shadow confounding,
Come the sea noises pounding, pounding,
Perpetual somnambular beat
That shakes the hard ground under my feet.
That sound in the dark long years since wrought
A danger in our fathers' thought.
It will come hereafter, perturbing the dream
Of who of our children may be or seem.
They'll turn on their beds in the night unstarred
When another Northeaster's breathing hard,
And their thoughts will fumble with imminent,
       strange,
Ancient uproar of things that change.
Slowly, slowly, the pebble is ground
In the tide-rolled shingle nearer the round.
Slowly, slowly, the silver arc
Of the new beach shapes in the fog-shot dark.
Slowly, slowly, the cliff's cut under,
The channel is filled, and the sand bars sunder
Slowly, slowly, with thunderous, numbing
Throb of a thing not known, becoming.

The statesmen always bungle
They see it in black and white.
But the singers are singing the people out of the
           jungle
Into the light.

Only song can win them
"Peace they were parted from,"
And voices with the beauty of darkness in them—
And Kingdom come!

Stephen Vincent Benét

SELECTIONS

From JOHN BROWN'S BODY

INVOCATION

American muse, whose strong and diverse heart
So many men have tried to understand
But only made it smaller with their art,
Because you are as various as your land,

As mountainous-deep, as flowered with blue
        rivers,
Thirsty with deserts, buried under the snows,
As native as the shape of Navajo quivers,
And native, too, as the sea-voyaged rose.

Swift runner, never captured or subdued,
Seven-branched elk beside the mountain stream,
That half a hundred hunters have pursued
But never matched their bullets with the dream,

Where the great huntsmen failed, I set my sorry
And mortal snare for your immortal quarry.

You are the buffalo-ghost, the broncho-ghost
With dollar-silver in your saddle-horn,
The cowboys riding in from Painted Post,
The Indian arrow in the Indian corn,

[19]

And you are the clipped velvet of the lawns
Where Shropshire grows from Massachusetts
    sods,
The grey Maine rocks—and the war-painted
    dawns
That break above the Garden of the Gods,

The prairie-schooners crawling toward the ore
And the cheap car, parked by the station-door.

Where the skyscrapers lift their foggy plumes
Of stranded smoke out of a stony mouth
You are that high stone and its arrogant fumes,
And you are ruined gardens in the South

And bleak New England farms, so winter-white
Even their roofs look lonely, and the deep
The middle grainland where the wind of night
Is like all blind earth sighing in her sleep.

A friend, an enemy, a sacred hag
With two tied oceans in her medicine-bag.

They tried to fit you with an English song
And clip your speech into the English tale.
But, even from the first, the words went wrong,
The catbird pecked away the nightingale.

The homesick men begot high-cheekboned things
Whose wit was whittled with a different sound
And Thames and all the rivers of the kings
Ran into Mississippi and were drowned.

They planted England with a stubborn trust.
But the cleft dust was never English dust.

Stepchild of every exile from content
And all the disavouched, hard-bitten pack
Shipped overseas to steal a continent
With neither shirts nor honor to their back.

Pimping grandee and rump-faced regicide,
Apple-cheeked younkers from a windmill-square,
Puritans stubborn as the nails of Pride,
Rakes from Versailles and thieves from County
        Clare,

The black-robed priests who broke their hearts
        in vain
To make you God and France or God and Spain.

These were your lovers in your buckskin-youth.
And each one married with a dream so proud
He never knew it could not be the truth
And that he coupled with a girl of cloud.

[21]

And now to see you is more difficult yet
Except as an immensity of wheel
Made up of wheels, oiled with inhuman sweat
And glittering with the heat of ladled steel.

All these you are, and each is partly you,
And none is false, and none is wholly true.

So how to see you as you really are,
So how to suck the pure, distillate, stored
Essence of essence from the hidden star
And make it pierce like a riposting sword.

For, as we hunt you down, you must escape
And we pursue a shadow of our own
That can be caught in a magician's cape
But has the flatness of a painted stone.

Never the running stag, the gull at wing,
The pure elixir, the American thing.

And yet, at moments when the mind was hot
With something fierier than joy or grief,
When each known spot was an eternal spot
And every leaf was an immortal leaf,

I think that I have seen you, not as one,
But clad in diverse semblances and powers,
Always the same, as light falls from the sun,
And always different, as the differing hours.

Yet, through each altered garment that you wore,
The naked body, shaking the heart's core.

All day the snow fell on that Eastern town
With its soft, pelting, little, endless sigh
Of infinite flakes that brought the tall sky down
Till I could put my hands in the white sky

And taste cold scraps of heaven on my tongue
And walk in such a changed and luminous light
As gods inhabit when the gods are young.
All day it fell. And when the gathered night

Was a blue shadow cast by a pale glow
I saw you then, snow-image, bird of the snow.

And I have seen and heard you in the dry
Close-huddled furnace of the city street
When the parched moon was planted in the sky
And the limp air hung dead against the heat.

I saw you rise, red as that rusty plant,
Dizzied with lights, half-mad with senseless
            sound,
Enormous metal, shaking to the chant
Of a triphammer striking iron ground.

Enormous power, ugly to the fool,
And beautiful as a well-handled tool.

These, and the memory of that windy day
On the bare hills, beyond the last barbed wire,
When all the orange poppies bloomed one way
As if a breath would blow them into fire,

I keep forever, like the sea-lion's tusk
The broken sailor brings away to land,
But when he touches it, he smells the musk,
And the whole sea lies hollow in his hand.

So, from a hundred visions, I make one,
And out of darkness build my mocking sun.

And should that task seem fruitless in the eyes
Of those a different magic sets apart
To see through the ice-crystal of the wise
No nation but the nation that is Art,

Their words are just. But when the birchbark-
      call
Is shaken with the sound that hunters make,
The moose comes plunging through the forest-
      wall
Although the rifle waits beside the lake.

Art has no nations—but the mortal sky
Lingers like gold in immortality.

This flesh was seeded from no foreign grain
But Pennsylvania and Kentucky wheat,
And it has soaked in California rain
And five years tempered in New England sleet

To strive at last, against an alien proof
And by the changes of an alien moon,
To build again that blue, American roof
Over a half-forgotten battle-tune

And call unsurely, from a haunted ground,
Armies of shadows and the shadow-sound.

In your Long House there is an attic-place
Full of dead epics and machines that rust,
And there, occasionally, with casual face,
You come awhile to stir the sleepy dust;

Neither in pride nor mercy, but in vast
Indifference at so many gifts unsought,
The yellowed satins, smelling of the past,
And all the loot the lucky pirates brought.

I only bring a cup of silver air,
Yet, in your casualness, receive it there.

Receive the dream too haughty for the breast,
Receive the words that should have walked as
        bold

[25]

As the storm walks along the mountain-crest
And are like beggars whining in the cold.

The maimed presumption, the unskilful skill,
The patchwork colors, fading from the first,
And all the fire that fretted at the will
With such a barren ecstasy of thirst.

Receive them all—and should you choose to touch
          them
With one slant ray of quick, American light,
Even the dust will have no power to smutch them,
Even the worst will glitter in the night.

If not—the dry bones littered by the way
May still point giants toward their golden prey.

THE YEARS RIDE OUT

The years ride out from the world like couriers
          gone to a throne
That is too far for treaty, or, as it may be, too
          proud;
The years marked with a star, the years that are
          skin and bone.
The years ride into the night like envoys sent to
          a cloud.

Perhaps they dismount at last, by some iron ring
 in the skies,
Dismount and tie their stallions and walk with an
 armored tread
Where an outlaw queen of the air receives strange
 embassies
Under a tree of wisdom, between the quick and
 the dead.

Perhaps they are merely gone, as the white foam
 flies from the bit,
But the sparkling noise of their riding is ever in
 our ears.—
The men who came to the maze without fore-
 knowledge of it,
The losers and the finders, under the riding years.

They pass, and the finders lose, the losers find for
 a space.
There are love and hate and delusion and all the
 tricks of the maze.
There are always losers and finders. There is no
 abiding-place
And the years are unreturning. But, here and
 there, there were days.

Days when the sun so shone that the statue gave
 its cry

And a bird shook wings or a woman walked with
a certain mirth,
When the staff struck out a spring from the stones
that had long been dry,
And the plough as before moved on from the hilltop, but its share had opened the earth.

So the bird is caught for an instant, and so the
bird escapes.
The years are not halted by it. The losers and
finders wait.
The years move on toward the sunset, the tall,
far-trafficking shapes,
Each with a bag of news to lay at a ghostly gate.

Riders shaking the heart with the hoofs that will
not cease,
Will you never lie stretched in marble, the hands
crossed over the breast,
Some with hounds at your feet to show that you
passed in peace,
And some with your feet on lions?
It is time that you were at rest.

JUBILI, JUBILO!

Sherman's buzzin' along to de sea,
Jubili, Jubilo!

Sherman's buzzin' along to de sea,
Like Moses ridin' on a bumblebee,
Settin' de prisoned and de humble free!
Hit's de year of Jubilo!

Massa was de whale wid de big inside,
Jubili, Jubilo!
Massa was de lion and de lion's hide.
But de Lord God smacked him in his hardheart
        pride,
And de whale unswallered, and de lion died!
Hit's de year of Jubilo!

Oh, hit don't matter if you's black or tan,
Jubili, Jubilo!
Hit don't matter if you's black or tan,
When you hear de noise of de freedom-ban'
You's snatched baldheaded to de Promise Lan',
Hit's de year of Jubilo!

Oh, hit don't matter if you pine or ail,
Jubili, Jubilo!
Hit don't matter if you pine or ail,
Hit don't matter if you's been in jail,
De Lord's got mercy for vour mumblin' tale!
Hit's de year of Jubilo!

Every nigger's gwine to own a mule,
Jubili, Jubilo!

Every nigger's gwine to own a mule,
An' live like Adam in de Golden Rule,
An' send his chillun to de white-folks' school!
In de year of Jubilo!

Fall down on your knees and bless de Lord,
Jubili, Jubilo!
Fall down on your knees and bless de Lord,
Dat chased old Pharaoh wid a lightnin'-sword,
And rose up Izzul fum de withered gourd,
Hit's de year of Jubilo!

Shout thanksgivin' and shout it loud!
Jubili, Jubilo!
Shout thanksgivin' and shout it loud,
We was dead and buried in de Lazrus-shroud,
But de Lord came down in a glory-cloud,
An' He gave us Jubilo!

JOHN BROWN'S BODY LIES
A-MOULDERING IN THE GRAVE

John Brown's body lies a-mouldering in the grave.
Spread over it the bloodstained flag of his song,
For the sun to bleach, the wind and the birds to
tear,
The snow to cover over with a pure fleece
And the New England cloud to work upon

With the grey absolution of its slow, most lilac-
	smelling rain,
Until there is nothing there
That ever knew a master or a slave
Or, brooding on the symbol of a wrong,
Threw down the irons in the field of peace.
John Brown is dead, he will not come again,
A stray ghost-walker with a ghostly gun.
Let the strong metal rust
In the enclosing dust
And the consuming coal
That was the furious soul
And still like iron groans,
Anointed with the earth,
Grow colder than the stones
While the white roots of grass and little weeds
Suck the last hollow wildfire from the singing
	bones.

Bury the South together with this man,
Bury the bygone South
Bury the minstrel with the honey-mouth,
Bury the broadsword virtues of the clan,
Bury the unmachined, the planters' pride,
The courtesy and the bitter arrogance,
The pistol-hearted horsemen who could ride
Like jolly centaurs under the hot stars.
Bury the whip, bury the branding-bars,
Bury the unjust thing

That some tamed into mercy, being wise,
But could not starve the tiger from its eyes
Or make it feed where beasts of mercy feed.
Bury the fiddle-music and the dance,
The sick magnolias of the false romance
And all the chivalry that went to seed
Before its ripening.

And with these things, bury the purple dream
Of the America we have not been,
The tropic empire, seeking the warm sea,
The last foray of aristocracy
Based not on dollars or initiative
Or any blood for what that blood was worth
But on a certain code, a manner of birth,
A certain manner of knowing how to live,

The pastoral rebellion of the earth
Against machines, against the Age of Steam,
The Hamiltonian extremes against the Franklin
            mean,
The genius of the land
Against the metal hand,
The great, slave-driven bark,
Full-oared upon the dark,
With gilded figurehead,
With fetters for the crew
And spices for the few,

The passion that is dead,
The pomp we never knew,
Bury this, too.

Bury this destiny unmanifest,
This system broken underneath the test,
Beside John Brown and though he knows his
        enemy is there
He is too full of sleep at last to care.

He was a stone, this man who lies so still,
A stone flung from a sling against a wall,
A sacrificial instrument of kill,
A cold prayer hardened to a musket-ball:
And yet, he knew the uses of a hill,
And he must have his justice, after all.

He was a lover of certain pastoral things,
He had the shepherd's gift.
When he walked at peace, when he drank from
        the watersprings,
His eyes would lift

To see God, robed in a glory, but sometimes, too,
Merely the sky,
Untroubled by wrath or angels, vacant and blue,
Vacant and high.

He knew not only doom but the shape of the land,
Reaping and sowing.
He could take a lump of any earth in his hand
And feel the growing.
He was a farmer, he didn't think much of towns,
The wheels, the vastness.
He liked the wide fields, the yellows, the lonely
      browns,
The black ewe's fastness.

Out of his body grows revolving steel,
Out of his body grows the spinning wheel
Made up of wheels, the new, mechanic birth,
No longer bound by toil
To the unsparing soil
Or the old furrow-line,
The great, metallic beast
Expanding West and East,
His heart a spinning coil,
His juices burning oil,
His body serpentine.
Out of John Brown's strong sinews the tall sky-
      scrapers grow,
Out of his heart the chanting buildings rise,
Rivet and girder, motor and dynamo,
Pillar of smoke by day and fire by night,
The steel-faced cities reaching at the skies,
The whole enormous and rotating cage

Hung with hard jewels of electric light,
Smoky with sorrow, black with splendor, dyed
Whiter than damask for a crystal bride
With metal suns, the engine-handed Age,
The genie we have raised to rule the earth,
Obsequious to our will
But servant-master still,
The tireless serf already half a god—

Touch the familiar sod
Once, then gaze at the air
And see the portent there,
With eyes for once washed clear
Of worship and of fear:
There is its hunger, there its living thirst,
There is the beating of the tremendous heart
You cannot read for omens,
                              Stand apart
From the loud crowd and look upon the flame
Alone and steadfast, without praise or blame.
This is the monster and the sleeping queen
And both have roots stuck deep in your own
          mind,
This is reality that you have seen,
This is reality that made you blind.

So, when the crowd gives tongue
And prophets, old or young,

Bawl out their strange despair
Or fall in worship there,
Let them applaud the image or condemn
But keep your distance and your soul from them,
And, if the heart within your breast must burst
Like a cracked crucible and pour its steel
White-hot before the white heat of the wheel,
Strive to recast once more
That attar of the ore
In the strong mold of pain
Till it is whole again,
And while the prophets shudder or adore
Before the flame, hoping it will give ear,
If you at last must have a word to say,
Say neither, in their way,
"It is a deadly magic and accursed,"
Nor "It is blest," but only "It is here."

Robert P. Tristram Coffin

EYES ARE LIT UP

Someone whom no man can see
Is lighting candles in the tree.

Star by star, on every bough
There is a taper burning now.

Quietly, the forest through,
Eyes are lit up, two by two.

The silky moles and velvet mice
Have eyes as sharp as cracks in ice.

Dark-lanterns of the owls begin
To burn like emeralds and sin.

The raccoon built of hidden wire
Prowls by the glow of his brain-fire.

Herons stand as still as years
And see the fish swim through their tears.

All the creatures of the night
Are busy being their own light.

A BOY, A LAKE, A SUN

My little boy, the vast, still lake,
　And the big low sun
Keep each other company,
　Now the day is done.

The child is quiet, and his curls
　Are full of evening light,
He sits in utter confidence
　On the edge of night.

A little golden bubble cast
　Up from eternity,
The sun is just as much his friend
　As the evening bee.

He does not know that he is small
　Or different or apart,
The sun is not a grander thing
　Than a daisy's heart.

But he is pleased to have me come
　And moves to let me sit
Beside him and the setting sun,
　And I am proud of it.

COUNTRY CHURCH

He could not separate the thought
Of God from daisies white and hot
In blinding thousands by a road,
Or dandelion disks that glowed
Like little suns upon the ground.
Holiness was like the sound
Of thousands of tumultuous bees
In full-blossomed apple trees,
Or it was smell of standing grain,
Or robins singing up a rain.

For the church he went to when
He was eight and nine and ten,
And good friends with the trees and sun,
Was a small white country one.
The caraway's lace parasols
Brushed the clapboards of its walls,
The grass flowed round it east and west,
And one blind had a robin's nest.
Before the sermon was half over,
It turned to fragrance of red clover.

May and June and other weather
And farmers' wives came in together,
At every window swung a bough,
Always, far off, someone's cow
Lowed and lowed at every pause.
The rhythms of the mighty laws
That keep men going, to their graves,
Were no holier than the waves
The wind made in the tasselled grass
A small boy saw through window glass.

STRANGE HOLINESS

There is a strange holiness around
Our common days on common ground.

I have heard it in the birds
Whose voices reach above all words,

Going upward, bars on bars,
Until they sound as high as stars.

I have seen it in the snake,
A flowing jewel in the brake.

It has sparkled in my eyes
In luminous breath of fireflies.

I have come upon its track
Where trilliums curled their petals back.

I have seen it flash in under
The towers of the midnight thunder.

Once, I met it face to face
In a fox pressed by the chase.

He came down the road on feet
Quiet and fragile, light as heat.

He had a fish still wet and bright
In his slender jaws held tight.

His ears were conscious, whetted darts,
His eyes had small flames in their hearts.

The preciousness of life and breath
Glowed through him as he outran death.

Strangeness and secrecy and pride
Ran rippling down his golden hide.

His beauty was not meant for me,
With my dull eyes, so close to see.

Unconscious of me, rapt, alone,
He came, and then stopped still as stone.

His eyes went out as in a gust,
His beauty crumbled into dust.

There was but a ruin there,
A hunted creature, stripped and bare.

Then he faded at one stroke
Like a dingy, melting smoke.

But there his fish lay like a key
To the bright, lost mystery.

FIREFLIES IN A GRAVEYARD

No one would notice this small cemetery
By day, there are so many cows to see
And furrows running up to meet the sky;
Most people have forgotten it is there.
But twilight makes it like the Milky Way
With myriads of hazy fireflies;
They come and go like coals the wind breathes on.
The light of their small, instant aureoles
Lights up the gravestones. Folks remember then
The way which all of us are bound to go.

You might suppose the fireflies' congregation
Had nothing in the way of warning in it,
But happened there because the grass was thick.
You must not be too sure, though; little flies
And birds all guileless, starry innocence
Have preached before to men, and city walls
Have fallen down before their eloquence.
It is good to know that there are graveyards
A stone's throw from the beds folks love upon,
A quiet place, with footprints all one way.

THE PINES

Behind the barn was mystery,
The pine trees there were like the sea
When wind was up; but it was more
Than waves upon an unseen shore
That made the boy's heart burn and sing.
He knew well there was a thing
In that spot which bound in one
All splendid things from sun to sun—
Amber jewels of roosters' eyes,
The floating beads of golden flies,
The rainbow's lintel of brief light
Arched across the door of night,
A duck's white feather like a flower
On a pool left by a shower,
The hot sound, steady, small, and keen,
Of August mowing by machine.
The cool sound of a scythe. The small
Madness of the cricket's call,
The sudden smell of apples in
October twilight from a bin,
The pleasure, lonely and immense,
Of the hearth-cat's confidence.

The pines behind the barn somehow
Joined the lowing of a cow
To the moon that marched through crowds
Of angels of fair-weather clouds.
The pines possessed the ancient right
Of opening doorways in the night
To let the day and cockcrow through,
They built a fire in the dew,
Laid the hand of East in West's,
Filled the eggs in robins' nests
With thunder rolling deep below
The earth at night. They mingled snow
Of Junetime daisies with December's,
And built the roses in the embers.

It took a boy of ten to see
Such a tremendous unity.

George Dillon

THE DEAD ELM ON THE
HILLTOP

This tree was burned by lightning to its root
In an October tempest many years ago now.
I can remember the lovely range of its bough,
Its scattered fruit,

Its voice as of waters on an invisible shore,
And the veined leaves transparent against the sky:
And so I have thought this tree could not die till
      I die.
Yet April comes no more

In a tall cloud of bronze to the top of the hill,
And summer stands no more in singing green,
And autumn, returning like a murderer to the
      scene,
Finds nothing left to kill.

MEMORY OF LAKE SUPERIOR

I know a country of bright anonymous beaches
Where the sand sleeps unprinted till it is stone.
Granite grows loud among the hills and ditches
Of the blown water when the water is blown.

Up on the mountain the sky is everywhere,
The lake fallen hugely underfoot as if
Into the bottom of a well of air,
The island upon it little as a leaf.

The woods are dark with the rank lace of hem-
      lock and pine,
Beech, birch, and balsam, and the shadow of
      these.
There are mushrooms, and thimbleberries sweeter
      than wine,
And a far noise of wind in the tops of the trees.

That country was all the knowledge I shall ever
      learn;
It was all the wisdom I shall ever have.
It was there I looked for the driftwood boughs
      that burn
In colours like a memory of the wave.

It was there I looked along the forest floor
For the grey feather of the grouse's wing.
It was there I learned to look for nothing more,
Looking into the sea-blue eyes of spring.

THE NOISE OF LEAVES

Alive in space against his will,
A man may find along his way
Some loveliness to live for still:

He falls upon the earth in May
And hides his face from the cold moon
Whose beauty mocks him when he grieves,
And hears the birds subside, and soon
Only the noise of blowing leaves,

And wonders why his heart grows light
To hear the soft contagion spread
From tree to tree across the night.
He knows that even the joinless dead
Are not so lonely where they sprawl,
Yet knows that he is not alone—

He clings to something after all,
Stretched on a flying flowering stone.

John Gould Fletcher

WHIRLPOOLS OF PURPLE

From IRRADIATIONS

Whirlpools of purple and gold,
Winds from the mountains of cinnabar,
Lacquered mandarin moments, palanquins sway-
       ing and balancing
Amid the vermilion pavilions, against the jade
       balustrades.
Glint of the glittering wings of dragon flies in the
       light:
Silver filaments, golden flakes settled downwards.

sees not just color

Crooked, crawling tide with long wet fingers
Clutching at the gritty beach in the roar and
    spurt of spray,
Tide of gales, drunken tide, lava-burst of breakers,
Black ships plunge upon you from sea to sea
    away.

Shattering tide, tide of winds, tide of the long
    still winter,
What matter though ships fail, men sink, there
    vanish glory?
War-clouds shall hurl their stinging sleet upon
    our last adventure,
Night-winds shall brokenly whisper our bitter,
    tragic story.

DOWN THE MISSISSIPPI

I. EMBARKATION

Dull masses of dense green,
The forests range their sombre platforms;
Between them silently, like a spirit,
The river finds its own mysterious path.

Loosely the river sways out, backward, forward,
Always fretting the outer side;
Shunning the invisible focus of each crescent,
Seeking to spread into shining loops over fields.

Like an enormous serpent, dilating, uncoiling
Displaying a broad scaly back of earth-smeared
      gold;
Swaying out sinuously between the dull motion-
      less forests,
As molten metal might glide down the lip of a
      vase of dark bronze;

It goes, while the steamboat drifting out upon it,
Seems now to be floating not only outwards but
      upwards;

In the flight of a petal detached and gradually
      moving skyward
Above the pink explosion of the calyx of the
      dawn.

II. HEAT

As if the sun had trodden down the sky,
Until it holds living air no more, but only humid
      vapor,
Heat pressing upon earth with irresistible languor,
Turns all the solid forest into half-liquid smudge.

The heavy clouds like cargo-boats strain slowly
      against its current;
And the flickering of the heat-haze is like the
      thunder of ten thousand paddles
Against the heavy wall of the horizon, pale blue
      and utterly windless,
Whereon the sun hangs motionless, a brassy disk
      of flame.

III. FULL MOON

Flinging its arc of silver bubbles, quickly shifts
      the moon
From side to side of us as we go down its path;
I sit on the deck at midnight and watch it slipping
      and sliding,

Under my tilted chair, like a thin film of spilt
    water.

It is weaving a river of light to take the place of
    this river;
A river where we shall drift all night, then come
    to rest in its shallows;
And then I shall wake from my drowsiness and
    look down from some dim treetop
Over white lakes of cotton, like moonfields on
    every side.

IV. THE MOON'S ORCHESTRA

When the moon lights up
Its dull red campfire through the trees;
And floats out, like a white balloon,
Into the blue cup of the night, borne by a casual
    breeze;
The moon-orchestra then begins to stir.
Jiggle of fiddles commence their crazy dance in
    the darkness:
Crickets churr
Against the stark reiteration of the rusty flutes
    which frogs
Puff at from rotted logs
In the swamp.
And then the moon begins her dance of frozen
    pomp

Over the lightly quivering floor of the flat and
        mournful river.
Her white feet slightly twist and swirl.
She is a mad girl
In an old unlit ballroom
Whose walls, half-guessed at through the gloom,
Are hung with the rusty crape of stark black
        cypresses
Which show, through gaps and tatters, red stains
        half hidden away.

V. THE STEVEDORES

Frieze of warm bronze that glides with catlike
        movement
Over the gangplank poised and yet awaiting,
The sinewy thudding rhythm of forty shuffling
        feet
Falling like muffled drumbeats on the stillness.
O roll the cotton down,
Roll, roll the cotton down,
From the further side of Jordan,
O roll the cotton down!

And the river waits,
The river listens,
Chuckling its little banjo-notes that break with a
        flop on the stillness;

And by the low dark shed that holds the heavy
        freights,
Two lonely cypresses stand up and point with
        stiffened fingers
Far southward where a single chimney stands
        out aloof in the sky.

VI. NIGHT LANDING

After the whistle's roar has bellowed and
        shuddered,
Shaking the sleeping town and the somnolent
        river,
The deep-toned floating of the pilot's bell
Suddenly warns the engines.

They stop like heart-beats that abruptly stop,
The shore glides to us in a wide low curve.

And then—supreme revelation of the river—
The tackle is loosed—the long gangplank swings
        outwards—
And poised at the end of it, half-naked beneath
        the searchlight,
A blue-black negro with gleaming teeth waits for
        his chance to leap.

[63]

VII. THE SILENCE

There is a silence I carry about with me always;
A silence perpetual, for it is self-created;
A silence of heat, of water, of unchecked fruit-
        fulness
Through which each year the heavy harvests
        bloom, and burst and fall.

Deep, matted green silence of my South,
Often within the push and scorn of great cities,
I have seen that mile-wide waste of water sway-
        ing out to you,
And on its current glimmering, I am going to the
        sea.

There is a silence I have achieved: I have walked
        beyond its threshold;
I know it is without horizons, boundless, fathom-
        less, perfect.
And some day maybe, far away,
I will curl up in it at last and sleep an endless
        sleep.

Robert Frost

STOPPING BY WOODS
ON A SNOWY EVENING

Whose woods these are I think I know.
His house is in the village though;
He will not see me stopping here
To watch his woods fill up with snow.

My little horse must think it queer
To stop without a farmhouse near
Between the woods and frozen lake
The darkest evening of the year.

He gives his harness bells a shake
To ask if there is some mistake.
The only other sound's the sweep
Of easy wind and downy flake.

The woods are lovely, dark and deep.
But I have promises to keep,
And miles to go before I sleep,
And miles to go before I sleep.

MENDING WALL

Something there is that doesn't love a wall,
That sends the frozen-ground-swell under it,
And spills the upper boulders in the sun;
And makes gaps even two can pass abreast.
The work of hunters is another thing:
I have come after them and made repair
Where they have left not one stone on a stone,
But they would have the rabbit out of hiding,
To please the yelping dogs. The gaps I mean,
No one has seen them made or heard them made,
But at spring mending-time we find them there.
I let my neighbour know beyond the hill;
And on a day we meet to walk the line
And set the wall between us once again.
We keep the wall between us as we go.
To each the boulders that have fallen to each.
And some are loaves and some so nearly balls
We have to use a spell to make them balance:
"Stay where you are until our backs are turned!"
We wear our fingers rough with handling them.
Oh, just another kind of out-door game,
One on a side. It comes to little more:
There where it is we do not need the wall:

He is all pine and I am apple orchard.
My apple trees will never get across
And eat the cones under his pines, I tell him.
He only says, "Good fences make good neigh-
  bours."
Spring is the mischief in me, and I wonder
If I could put a notion in his head:
"*Why* do they make good neighbours? Isn't it
Where there are cows? But here there are no
  cows.
Before I built a wall I'd ask to know
What I was walling in or walling out,
And to whom I was like to give offence.
Something there is that doesn't love a wall,
That wants it down." I could say "Elves" to him,
But it's not elves exactly, and I'd rather
He said it for himself. I see him there
Bringing a stone grasped firmly by the top
In each hand, like an old-stone savage armed.
He moves in darkness as it seems to me,
Not of woods only and the shade of trees.
He will not go behind his father's saying,
And he likes having thought of it so well
He says again, "Good fences make good neigh-
  bours."

[69]

She had no saying dark enough
    For the dark pine that kept
Forever trying the window-latch
    Of the room where they slept.

The tireless but ineffectual hands
    That with every futile pass
Made the great tree seem as a little bird
    Before the mystery of glass!

It never had been inside the room,
    And only one of the two
Was afraid in an oft-repeated dream
    Of what the tree might do.

Once when the snow of the year was beginning
      to fall,
We stopped by a mountain pasture to say, "Whose
      colt?"
A little Morgan had one forefoot on the wall,
The other curled at his breast. He dipped his head
And snorted at us. And then he had to bolt.
We heard the miniature thunder where he fled,
And we saw him, or thought we saw him, dim
      and grey,
Like a shadow against the curtain of falling flakes.
"I think the little fellow's afraid of the snow.
He isn't winter-broken. It isn't play
With the little fellow at all. He's running away.
I doubt if even his mother could tell him, 'Sakes,
It's only weather.' He'd think she didn't know!
Where is his mother? He can't be out alone."
And now he comes again with clatter of stone,
And mounts the wall again with whited eyes
And all his tail that isn't hair up straight.
He shudders his coat as if to throw off flies.
"Whoever it is that leaves him out so late,
When other creatures have gone to stall and bin,
Ought to be told to come and take him in."

THE SOUND OF TREES

I wonder about the trees.
Why do we wish to bear
Forever the noise of these
More than another noise
So close to our dwelling place?
We suffer them by the day
Till we lose all measure of pace,
And fixity in our joys,
And acquire a listening air.
They are that that talks of going
But never gets away;
And that talks no less for knowing,
As it grows wiser and older,
That now it means to stay.
My feet tug at the floor
And my head sways to my shoulder
Sometimes when I watch trees sway,
From the window or the door.
I shall set forth for somewhere,
I shall make the reckless choice
Some day when they are in voice
And tossing so as to scare
The white clouds over them on.
I shall have less to say,
But I shall be gone.

Robert Hillyer

REMOTE

The farthest country is Tierra del Fuego,
That is the bleakest and the loneliest land;
There are the echoing mountains of felspar,
And salt winds walking the empty sand.

This country remembers the birth of the moon
From a rocky rib of the young earth's side;
It heard the white-hot mountains bellow
Against the march of the first flood tide.

I lifted a shell by the grass-green breakers
And heard what no man has heard before,
The whisper of steam in the hot fern forest
And slow feet crunching the ocean floor.

I saw the slanted flash of a sea gull
When a sheaf of light poured over the clouds,
I heard the wind in the stiff dune grasses,
But I saw no sail and I heard no shrouds.

To a promontory of Tierra del Fuego
I climbed at noon and stretched my hand
Toward another country, remoter and bleaker.

[75]

LULLABY

The long canoe
Toward the shadowy shore,
One . . . two . . .
Three . . . four. . . .
The paddle dips,
Turns in the wake,
Pauses, then
Forward again.
Water drips
From the blade to the lake.
Nothing but that,
No sound of wings;
The owl and bat
Are velvet things.
No wind awakes,
No fishes leap,
No rabbits creep
Among the brakes.
The long canoe
At the shadowy shore,
One . . . two . . .
Three . . . four. . . .
A murmur now

Under the prow
Where the rushes bow
To let us through.
One . . . two . . .
Upon the shore,
Three . . . four . . .
Upon the lake,
No one's awake,
No one's awake,
One . . . two . . .
No one, not even you.

FOLK SONG

Now time has gathered to itself
    The lily and the rose,
To mould upon a dusty shelf
    Where no man knows.

Now all things lovely fail and wane,
    The tender petals close,
And in the dawn shall bloom again
    No lily, no rose.

Now from the garden of your face
    The lily and the rose
Are gathered to a dusty place
    Where no man knows.

FOLK SONG

The stars came, but her Love came never,
And standing there on the bank of the river,
"Come back!" she said to the waves of the river,
But they hurried away and they came back never.
"You come not back to the land of my lover,"
She said to the hurrying waves of the river,
"Then will I go with you, waves of the river,
To oceans far from the land of my lover."
Under the starlight the girl and the river
Hurry away and they come back never.

He who in spring's rebirth has put his trust
Now answers not to April or to May,
Nor sees the moon-white apple blossom sway,
Nor breathes its sweetness on the evening gust.
He who was first to climb the height of day
Lies full-length in the valley of the dust;
His sword sleeps in his hand, and it is rust;
His heart sleeps in his breast, and it is clay.
Brother, so mute among the fallen years,
We come at dayspring to your living tomb
That is the green earth, and we shed no tears,
Knowing that if you wander otherwhere
Soon will you give us gracious welcome there,
And if you perished, then we share your doom.

Amy Lowell

MERELY STATEMENT

You sent me a sprig of mignonette,
Cool-coloured, quiet, and it was wet
With green sea-spray, and the salt and the sweet
Mingled to a fragrance weary and discreet
As a harp played softly in a great room at sunset.

You said: "My sober mignonette
Will brighten your room and you will not forget."

But I have pressed your flower and laid it away
In a letter, tied with a ribbon knot.
I have not forgot.
But there is a passion-flower in my vase
Standing above a close-cleared space
In the midst of a jumble of papers and books.
The passion-flower holds my eyes,
And the light-under-light of its blue and purple
dyes
Is a hot surprise.
How then can I keep my looks
From the passion-flower leaning sharply over the
books?

When one has seen
The difficult magnificence of a queen
On one's table,
Is one able
To observe any colour in a mignonette?

I will not think of sunset, I crave the dawn,
With its rose-red light on the wings of a swan,
And a queen pacing slowly through the Parthenon,
Her dress a stare of purple between pillars of
        stone.

SUMMER NIGHT PIECE

The garden is steeped in moonlight,
Full to its high edges with brimming silver,
And the fish-ponds brim and darken
And run in little serpent lights soon extinguished.
Lily-pads lie upon the surface, beautiful as the
        tarnishings on frail old silver,
And the Harvest moon droops heavily out of the
        sky,
A ripe, white melon, intensely, magnificently,
        shining.
Your window is orange in the moonlight,
It glows like a lamp behind the branches of the
        old wistaria,
It burns like a lamp before a shrine,
The small, intimate, familiar shrine
Placed reverently among the bricks
Of a much-loved garden wall.

"I grasped a thread of silver; it cut me to the
   bone—
I reached for an apple; it was bleak as a stone—
I reached for a heart, and touched a raw blade—
And this was the bargain God had made
For a little gift of speech
Set a cubit higher than the common reach,
A debt running on until the fool is dead."

Carve a Pater Noster to put at his head
As a curse or a prayer,
And leave him there.

I must be mad, or very tired,
When the curve of a blue bay beyond a railroad
        track
Is shrill and sweet to me like the sudden spring-
        ing of a tune,
And the sight of a white church above thin trees
        in a city square
Amazes my eyes as though it were the Parthenon.
Clear, reticent, superbly final,
With the pillars of its portico refined to a cautious
        elegance,
It dominates the weak trees,
And the shot of its spire
Is cool, and candid,
Rising into an unresisting sky.
Strange meeting-house
Pausing a moment upon a squalid hilltop.
I watch the spire sweeping the sky,
I am dizzy with the movement of the sky,
I might be watching a mast
With its royals set full,
Straining before a two-reef breeze.
I might be sighting a tea-clipper,

Tacking into the blue bay,
Just back from Canton
With her hold full of green and blue porcelain,
And a Chinese coolie leaning over the rail
Gazing at the white spire
With dull, sea-spent eyes.

LILACS

Lilacs,
False blue,
White,
Purple,
Colour of lilac,
Your great puffs of flowers
Are everywhere in this my New England.
Among your heart-shaped leaves
Orange orioles hop like music-box birds and sing
Their little weak soft songs;
In the crooks of your branches
The bright eyes of song sparrows sitting on
            spotted eggs
Peer restlessly through the light and shadow
Of all Springs.
Lilacs in dooryards
Holding quiet conversations with an early moon;
Lilacs watching a deserted house
Settling sideways into the grass of an old road;
Lilacs, wind-beaten, staggering under a lopsided
            shock of bloom
Above a cellar dug into a hill.
You are everywhere.

You were everywhere.
You tapped the window when the preacher
preached his sermon,
And ran along the road beside the boy going to
school.
You stood by pasture-bars to give the cows good
milking,
You persuaded the housewife that her dishpan
was of silver
And her husband an image of pure gold.
You flaunted the fragrance of your blossoms
Through the wide doors of Custom Houses—
You, and sandal-wood, and tea,
Charging the noses of quill-driving clerks
When a ship was in from China.
You called to them: "Goose-quill men, goose-quill
men,
May is a month for flitting,"
Until they writhed on their high stools
And wrote poetry on their letter sheets behind
the propped-up ledgers.
Paradoxical New England clerks,
Writing inventories in ledgers, reading the "Song
of Solomon" at night,
So many verses before bed-time,
Because it was the Bible.
The dead fed you
Amid the slant stones of graveyards.
Pale ghosts who planted you

Came in the nighttime
And let their thin hair blow through your clus-
tered stems.
You are of the green sea,
And of the stone hills which reach a long distance.
You are of elm-shaded streets with little shops
where they sell kites and marbles,
You are of great parks where everyone walks and
nobody is at home.
You cover the blind sides of greenhouses
And lean over the top to say a hurry-word through
the glass
To your friends, the grapes, inside.

Lilacs,
False blue,
White,
Purple,
Colour of lilac,
You have forgotten your Eastern origin,
The veiled women with eyes like panthers,
The swollen, aggressive turbans of jewelled
Pashas.
Now you are a very decent flower,
A reticent flower,
A curiously clear-cut, candid flower,
Standing beside clean doorways,
Friendly to a house-cat and a pair of spectacles,
Making poetry out of a bit of moonlight

And a hundred or two sharp blossoms.
Maine knows you,
Has for years and years;
New Hampshire knows you,
And Massachusetts
And Vermont.
Cape Cod starts you along the beaches to Rhode
        Island;
Connecticut takes you from a river to the sea.
You are brighter than apples,
Sweeter than tulips,
You are the great flood of our souls
Bursting above the leaf-shapes of our hearts,
You are the smell of all Summers,
The love of wives and children,
The recollection of the gardens of little children,
You are State Houses and Charters
And the familiar treading of the foot to and fro
        on a road it knows.
May is lilac here in New England,
May is a thrush singing "Sun-up!" on a tip-top
        ash-tree,
May is white clouds behind pine-trees
Puffed out and marching upon a blue sky.
May is a green as no other,
May is much sun through small leaves,
May is soft earth,
And apple-blossoms,
And windows open to a South wind.

May is a full light wind of lilac
From Canada to Narragansett Bay.

Lilacs,
False blue,
White,
Purple,
Colour of lilac,
Heart-leaves of lilac all over New England,
Roots of lilac under all the soil of New England,
Lilacs in me because I am New England,
Because my roots are in it,
Because my leaves are of it,
Because my flowers are for it,
Because it is my country
And I speak to it of itself
And sing of it with my own voice
Since certainly it is mine.

AFTERGLOW

Peonies
The strange pink colour of Chinese porcelains,
Wonderful—the glow of them.
But, my Dear, it is the pale blue larkspur
Which swings windily against my heart.
Other Summers—
And a cricket chirping in the grass.

Archibald MacLeish

BERNAL DIAZ' PREFACE TO HIS BOOK

From CONQUISTADOR

'That which I have myself seen and the fight-
    ing'. . . .

And I am an ignorant man: and this priest this
Gómara with the school-taught skip to his writing

The pompous Latin the appropriate feasts
The big names the imperial decorations
The beautiful battles and the brave deceased

The onward marches the wild Indian nations
The conquests sieges sorties wars campaigns
(And one eye always on the live relations)—

He with his famous history of New Spain—
This priest is a learned man: is not ignorant:
And I am poor: without gold: gainless:

My lands deserts in Guatemala: my fig-tree the
Spiked bush: my grapes thorns: my children
Half-grown: sons with beards: the big one

Breaking the small of his back in the brothel thills
And a girl to be married and all of them snarling
            at home
With the Indian look in their eyes like a cat
      killing:

And this Professor Francisco López de Gómara
Childless; not poor: and I am old: over eighty:
Stupid with sleepless nights: unused to the comb-
            ing of

Words clean of the wool while the tale waits:
And he is a youthful man: a sound one: lightened
            with
Good sleep: skilled in the pen's plaiting—

I am an ignorant old sick man: blind with the
Shadow of death on my face and my hands to
            lead me:
And he not ignorant: not sick—

                        but I

Fought in those battles! These were my own
            deeds!

These names he writes of mouthing them out as
          a man would
Names in Herodotus—dead and their wars to
          read—

These were my friends: these dead my com-
          panions:
I: Bernál Díaz: called del Castíllo:
Called in the time of my first fights El Galán:

I here in the turn of the day in the feel of
Darkness to come now: moving my chair with
          the change:
Thinking too much these times how the doves
          would wheel at

Evening over my youth and the air's strangeness:
Thinking too much of my old town of Medina
And the Spanish dust and the smell of the true
          rain:

I: poor: blind in the sun: I have seen
With these eyes those battles: I saw Montezúma:
I saw the armies of Mexico marching the leaning

Wind in their garments: the painted faces: the
          plumes
Blown on the light air: I saw that city:
I walked at night on those stones: in the shadowy
          rooms

I have heard the clink of my heel and the bats
        twittering:
I: poor as I am: I was young in that country:
These words were my life: these letters written

Cold on the page with the split ink and the shunt
        of the
Stubborn thumb: these marks at my fingers:
These are the shape of my own life . . .
                                and I hunted the

Unknown birds in the west with their beautiful
        wings!

Old men should die with their time's span:
The sad thing is not death: the sad thing

Is the life's loss out of earth when the living
        vanish:
All that was good in the throat: the hard going:
The marching singing in sunshine: the showery
        land:

The quick loves: the sleep: the waking: the blow-
        ing of
Winds over us: all this that we knew:
All this goes out at the end as the flowing of

Water carries the leaves down: and the few—
Three or four there are of us still that remember
       it—
Perish: and that time's stopt like a stale tune:

And the bright young masters with their bitter
       treble
Understanding it all like an old game!
And the pucker of art on their lips like the pip
       of a lemon!—

'The tedious veteran jealous of his fame!'
What is my fame or the fame of these my
       companions?
Their tombs are the bellies of Indians: theirs are
       the shameful

Graves in the wild earth: in the Godless sand:
None know the place of their bones: as for mine
Strangers will dig my grave in a stony land:

Even my sons have the strangeness of dark kind
       in them:
Indian dogs will bark at dusk by my sepulchre:
What is my fame! But those days: the shine of the

Sun in that time: the wind then: the step
Of the moon over those leaf-fallen nights: the
       sleet in the
Dry grass: the smell of the dust where we slept—

[101]

These things were real: these suns had heat in
    them:
This was brine in the mouth: bitterest foam:
Earth: water to drink: bread to be eaten—

Not the sound of a word like the writing of
    Gómara:
Not a past time: a year: the name of a
Battle lost—'and the Emperor Charles came home

'That year: and that was the year the same
'They fought in Flanders and the Duke was
    hung—'
The dates of empire: the dry skull of fame!

No but our lives: the days of our lives: we were
    young then:
The strong sun was standing in deep trees:
We drank at the springs: the thongs of our swords
    unslung to it:

We saw that city on the inland sea:
Towers between: and the green-crowned
    Montezúma
Walking the gardens of shade: and the staggering
    bees

And the girls bearing the woven baskets of bloom
    on their

Black hair: their breasts alive: and the hunters
Shouldering dangling herons with their ruffled
    plumes:

We were the first that found that famous country:
We marched by a king's name: we crossed the
    sierras:
Unknown hardships we suffered: hunger:

Death by the stone knife: thirst: we fared by the
Bitter streams: we came at last to that water:
Towers were steep upon the fluttering air:

We were the lords of it all . . .
                        Now time has taught us:
Death has mastered us most: sorrow and pain
Sickness and evil days are our lives' lot:

Now even the time of our youth has been taken:
Now are our deeds words: our lives chronicles:
Afterwards none will think of the night rain. . . .

How shall a man endure the will of God and the
Days and the silence!
                    In the world before us
Neither in Cuba nor the isles beyond—

Not Fonséca himself the sagging whore—
Not the Council the Audience even the Indians—

Knew of a land to the west: they skirted the
Floridas:

They ran the islands on the bare-pole winds:
They touched the Old Main and the midland
shores:
They saw the sun go down at the gulf's beginning:

None had sailed to the west and returned till
Córdova:
I went in that ship: Alvarez handled her:
Trusting to luck: keeping the evening before him:

Sighting after the third week land
And no report of a land there in that ocean:
The Indians clean: wearing the delicate bands:

Cape Catoche we called it: 'conës catoche'—
So they cried to us over the sea flood:
Many idols they had for their devotion

Some of women: some coupled in sodomy
So we sailed on: we came to Campéchë:
There by the sweet pool they kindled the wood-
fire:

Words they were saying like 'Castilán' in their
speech:

They warned us by signs to be gone when the
      logs charred:
So we turned from them down to the smooth
      beaches:

The boats followed us close in: we departed:
Afterwards there was a *nortë* with fine haze:
We stood for Potonchán through the boil of the
      narrows:

There they attacked us crossing the green of the
      maize fields:
Me they struck thrice and they killed fifty
And all were hurt and two taken crazy with

Much pain and it blew and the dust lifted
And the thirst cracked the tongues in our mouths
      and before us the
Sea-corrupted pools where the river drifts:

And we turned back and the wind drove us to
      Florida:
There in the scooped sand in the withered bed—
There by the sea they encountered us threatening
      war:

So we returned to the islands half dead:
And Córdova did die: and we wrote to
      Velásquez—
Diégo the Governor—writing it out: and we said—

'Excellence: there are lands in the west: the pass is
'Clean sailing: the scuts of the men are covered:
'The houses are masonry: gold they have: baskets

'Painted with herbs: the women are chaste in love'—
Much else of the kind I cannot remember:
And Velásquez took the credit for this discovery:

And all we had was our wounds: and enough of them:
And Fonséca Bishop of Búrgos (for so he was called)
President of the Council: he wrote to the Emperor

Telling the wonderful news in a mule's volley
And not a word of our deeds or our pains or our battles:
And Charles gone: and Joanna the poor queen stalled

In Tordesíllas shaking the peas in rattle:
And Barbarossa licking his chin in Algiers:
And trouble enough in Spain with all that

And the Cardinal dying and Sicily over the ears—
Trouble enough without new lands to be conquered and
Naked Indians taken and wild sheep sheared:

But as for us that returned from that westward
            country—
We could not lie in our towns for the sound of
            the sea:
We could not rest at all in our thoughts: we were
            young then:

We looked to the west: we remembered the
            foreign trees
Borne out on the tide from the unknown rivers
And the clouds like hills in the air our eyes had
            seen:

And Grijálva sailed next and we that were living—
We that had gear to our flesh and the gold to find
And an old pike in the stall with the haft to it
            slivered—

We signed on and we sailed by the first tide:
And we fought at Potonchán that voyage: I
            remember
The locusts covered the earth like a false shine
            to it:

They flew with a shrill sound like the arrow stem:
Often we took the whir of the darts for the
            locusts:
Often we left our shields from our mouths as they
            came:

I remember our fighting was much marred by the
       locusts:
And that voyage we came to the river Tabasco:
We saw the nets as we came in and the smoke
       of the

Sea over the bar: and we filled the casks there:
There first we heard of the farther land—
'Colúa' they said 'Méjico'—we that were asking
       the

Gold there on that shore on the evening sand—
'Colúa' they said: pointing on toward the sunset:
They made a sign on the air with their solemn
       hands:

Afterward: north: on the sea: and the ships
       running
We saw the steep snow mountain on the sky:
We stared as dream-awakened men in wonder:

And that voyage it was we came to the Island:
Well I remember the shore and the sound of that
       place
And the smoke smell on the dunes and the wind
       dying:

Well I remember the walls and the rusty taste
       of the

New-spilled blood in the air: many among us
Seeing the priests with their small and arrogant
        faces:

Seeing the dead boys' breasts and the idols hung
        with the
Dried shells of the hearts like the husks of cicadas
And their human eyeballs and their painted
        tongues

Cried out to the Holy Mother of God for it:
And some that stood there bore themselves the
        stone:
And some were eaten of wild beasts of their
        bodies:

And none of us all but had his heart foreknown
        the
Evil to come would have turned from the land
        then:
But the lives of men are covered and not shown—

Only late to the old at their time's ending
The land shows backward and the way is there:
And the next day we sailed and the sea was
        against us

And our bread was dirty with weevils and grown
        scarce and the

Rains began and the beans stank in the ovens
And we soldiers were thoroughly tired of sea-
          faring:

So we returned from that voyage with God's love:
And they talked about nothing else in the whole
          of Cuba:
And gentlemen sold their farms to go on dis-
          coveries:

And we that had fought in the marshes with no
          food—
We sat by the palms in the square in the green
          gloaming
With the delicate girls on our knees and the night
          to lose:

We that had fought in those lands. . . .
                    and the eloquent Gómara:
The quilled professors: the taught tongues of
          fame:
What have they written of us: the poor soldiers:

We that were wounded often for no pay:
We that died and were dumped cold in the bread
          sacks:
Bellies up: the birds at us: floating for days

And none remembering which it was that was
        dead there
Whether of Búrgos or Yúste or Villalár:
Where have they written our names? What have
        they said of us?

They call the towns for the kings that bear no
        scars:
They keep the names of the great for time to stare
        at—
The bishops rich-men generals cocks-at-arms:

Those with the glaze in their eyes and the fine
        bearing:
The born leaders of men: the resonant voices:
They give them the lands for their tombs: they
        call it *America!*

(And who has heard of Vespucci in this soil
Or down by the lee of the coast or toward the
        Havana?)
And we that fought here: that with heavy toil

Earthed up the powerful cities of this land—
What are we? When will our fame come?
An old man in a hill town
                        a handful of
Dust under the dry grass at Otúmba

[111]

Unknown names
               hands vanished
                          faces
Many gone from the day
                     unspeakable numbers
Lives forgotten
            deeds honored in strangers

'That which I have myself seen and the fight-
    ing'. . . .

Edna St. Vincent Millay

AUTUMN CHANT

Now the autumn shudders
   In the rose's root.
Far and wide the ladders
   Lean among the fruit.

Now the autumn clambers
   Up the trellised frame,
And the rose remembers
   The dust from which it came.

Brighter than the blossom
   On the rose's bough
Sits the wizened orange,
   Bitter berry now;

Beauty never slumbers;
   All is in her name;
But the rose remembers
   The dust from which it came.

TO THE NOT IMPOSSIBLE HIM

How shall I know, unless I go
    To Cairo and Cathay,
Whether or not this blessed spot
    Is blest in every way?

Now it may be, the flower for me
    Is this beneath my nose;
How shall I tell, unless I smell
    The Carthaginian rose?

The fabric of my faithful love
    No power shall dim or ravel
Whilst I stay here,—but oh, my dear,
    If I should ever travel!

SONNET

Here is a wound that never will heal, I know,
Being wrought not of a dearness and a death,
But of a love turned ashes and the breath
Gone out of beauty; never again will grow
The grass on that scarred acre, though I sow
Young seed there yearly and the sky bequeath
Its friendly weathers down, far underneath
Shall be such bitterness of an old woe.

That April should be shattered by a gust,
That August should be levelled by a rain,
I can endure, and that the lifted dust
Of man should settle to the earth again;
But that a dream can die, will be a thrust
Between my ribs forever of hot pain.

Edwin Arlington Robinson

THE SHEAVES

Where long the shadows of the wind had rolled,
Green wheat was yielding to the change assigned:
And as by some vast magic undivined
The world was turning slowly into gold.
Like nothing that was ever bought or sold
It waited there, the body and the mind;
And with a mighty meaning of a kind
That tells the more the more it is not told.

So in a land where all days are not fair,
Fair days went on till on another day
A thousand golden sheaves were lying there,
Shining and still, but not for long to stay—
As if a thousand girls with golden hair
Might rise from where they slept and go away.

THE MASTER

(LINCOLN)

A flying word from here and there
Had sown the name at which we sneered,
But soon the name was everywhere,
To be reviled and then revered:
A presence to be loved and feared,
We cannot hide it, or deny
That we, the gentlemen who jeered,
May be forgotten by and by.

He came when days were perilous
And hearts of men were sore beguiled;
And having made his note of us,
He pondered and was reconciled.
Was ever master yet so mild
As he, and so untamable?
We doubted, even when he smiled,
Not knowing what he knew so well.

He knew that undeceiving fate
Would shame us whom he served unsought;
He knew that he must wince and wait—

The jest of those for whom he fought;
He knew devoutly what he thought
Of us and of our ridicule;
He knew that we must all be taught
Like little children in a school.

We gave a glamour to the task
That he encountered and saw through,
But little of us did he ask,
And little did we ever do.
And what appears if we review
The season when we railed and chaffed?
It is the face of one who knew
That we were learning while we laughed.

The face that in our vision feels
Again the venom that we flung,
Transfigured to the world reveals
The vigilance to which we clung.
Shrewd, hallowed, harassed, and among
The mysteries that are untold,
The face we see was never young
Nor could it wholly have been old.

For he, to whom we had applied
Our shopman's test of age and worth,
Was elemental when he died,
As he was ancient at his birth:
The saddest among kings of earth,

Bowed with a galling crown, this man
Met rancor with a cryptic mirth,
Laconic—and Olympian.

The love, the grandeur, and the fame
Are bounded by the world alone;
The calm, the smouldering, and the flame
Of awful patience were his own:
With him they are forever flown
Past all our fond self-shadowings,
Wherewith we cumber the Unknown
As with inept, Icarian wings.

For we were not as other men:
'Twas ours to soar and his to see;
But we are coming down again,
And we shall come down pleasantly;
Nor shall we longer disagree
On what it is to be sublime,
But flourish in our perigee
And have one Titan at a time.

*—Supposed to have been written
not long after the Civil War.*

ISOLT OF THE WHITE HANDS

From Tristram

                    Yet there she gazed
Across the water, over the white waves,
Upon a castle that she had never seen,
And could not see, save as a phantom shape
Against a phantom sky.

                   He had been all,
And would be always all there was for her,
And he had not come back to her alive,
Not even to go again. It was like that
For women, sometimes, and might be so too often
For women like her. She hoped there were not
        many
Of them, or many of them to be, now knowing
More about that than about waves and foam,
And white birds everywhere, flying and flying;
Alone, with her white face and her gray eyes,
She watched them there till even her thoughts
        were white,
And there was nothing alive but white birds
        flying,
Flying, and always flying, and still flying,
And the white sunlight flashing on the sea.

MINIVER CHEEVY

Miniver Cheevy, child of scorn,
 Grew lean while he assailed the seasons;
He wept that he was ever born,
 And he had reasons.

Miniver loved the days of old
 When swords were bright and steeds were
  prancing;
The vision of a warrior bold
 Would set him dancing.

Miniver sighed for what was not,
 And dreamed, and rested from his labors;
He dreamed of Thebes and Camelot,
 And Priam's neighbors.

Miniver mourned the ripe renown
 That made so many a name so fragrant;
He mourned Romance, now on the town,
 And Art, a vagrant.

Miniver loved the Medici,
 Albeit he had never seen one;

He would have sinned incessantly
    Could he have been one.

Miniver cursed the commonplace
    And eyed a khaki suit with loathing;
He missed the mediaeval grace
    Of iron clothing.

Miniver scorned the gold he sought,
    But sore annoyed was he without it;
Miniver thought, and thought, and thought,
    And thought about it.

Miniver Cheevy, born too late,
    Scratched his head and kept on thinking;
Miniver coughed, and called it fate,
    And kept on drinking.

FLAMMONDE

The man Flammonde, from God knows where,
With firm address and foreign air,
With news of nations in his talk
And something royal in his walk,
With glint of iron in his eyes,
But never doubt, nor yet surprise,
Appeared, and stayed, and held his head
As one by kings accredited.

Erect, with his alert repose
About him, and about his clothes,
He pictured all tradition hears
Of what we owe to fifty years.
His cleansing heritage of taste
Paraded neither want nor waste;
And what he needed for his fee
To live, he borrowed graciously.

He never told us what he was,
Or what mischance, or other cause,
Had banished him from better days
To play the Prince of Castaways.
Meanwhile he played surpassing well

A part, for most, unplayable;
In fine, one pauses, half afraid
To say for certain that he played.

For that, one may as well forego
Conviction as to yes or no;
Nor can I say just how intense
Would then have been the difference
To several, who, having striven
In vain to get what he was given,
Would see the stranger taken on
By friends not easy to be won.

Moreover, many a malcontent
He soothed and found munificent;
His courtesy beguiled and foiled
Suspicion that his years were soiled;
His mien distinguished any crowd,
His credit strengthened when he bowed;
And women, young and old, were fond
Of looking at the man Flammonde.

There was a woman in our town
On whom the fashion was to frown;
But while our talk renewed the tinge
Of a long-faded scarlet fringe,
The man Flammonde saw none of that,
And what he saw we wondered at—

That none of us, in her distress,
Could hide or find our littleness.

There was a boy that all agreed
Had shut within him the rare seed
Of learning. We could understand,
But none of us could lift a hand.
The man Flammonde appraised the youth,
And told a few of us the truth;
And thereby, for a little gold,
A flowered future was unrolled.

There were two citizens who fought
For years and years, and over nought;
They made life awkward for their friends,
And shortened their own dividends.
The man Flammonde said what was wrong
Should be made right; nor was it long
Before they were again in line,
And had each other in to dine.

And these I mention are but four
Of many out of many more.
So much for them. But what of him—
So firm in every look and limb?
What small satanic sort of kink
Was in his brain? What broken link
Withheld him from the destinies
That came so near to being his?

What was he, when we came to sift
His meaning, and to note the drift
Of incommunicable ways
That make us ponder while we praise?
Why was it that his charm revealed
Somehow the surface of a shield?
What was it that we never caught?
What was he, and what was he not?

How much it was of him we met
We cannot ever know; nor yet
Shall all he gave us quite atone
For what was his, and his alone;
Nor need we now, since he knew best,
Nourish an ethical unrest:
Rarely at once will nature give
The power to be Flammonde and live.

We cannot know how much we learn
From those who never will return,
Until a flash of unforeseen
Remembrance falls on what has been.
We've each a darkening hill to climb;
And this is why, from time to time
In Tilbury Town, we look beyond
Horizons for the man Flammonde.

Leonora Speyer

MEASURE ME, SKY!

Measure me, sky!
Tell me I reach by a song
Nearer the stars;
I have been little so long.

Weigh me, high wind!
What will your wild scales record?
Profit of pain,
Joy by the weight of a word.

Horizon, reach out,
Catch at my hands, stretch me taut,
Rim of the world!
Widen my eyes by a thought.

Sky, be my depth,
Wind, be my tolerant height,
World, my heart's span—
Loneliness, wings for my flight!

AFFINITY

Her mouth was shaped to happy tunes
That flying, she let fall,
But when his silence mended them
She could not sing at all.

She could not fly without her tunes,
They were her only wings,
But there were pleasant ways to walk
Among sure-footed things.

She walks content, her hand in his;
But neither of them sings.

SAND-PIPINGS

1. GULLS

Strong wings in the stormy weather—
Gray stitches that hold
The raveling fabrics of sea and sky
Forever together!

2. STORM'S END

As if engraved upon the dawn,
The sleek gulls stand
Along the rim of an exhausted sea
That rumbles up the sand.

Amazing birds, untired and trim of wing,
Whose round unflinching eyes
Meet like a challenge the leaden-lidded sun
About to rise.

3. FOR A SPRING DAY

Here is no bud, no blade,
No young green thing;
This stark earth knows a meager spring.

Gulls are the only birds,
And thin their cries,
Bleak winter in their frosty eyes.

Somewhere, are fields and boughs,
A hill, a brook;
I would not lift my head to look

From this wind-shapen dune,
This stern still place,
This sea that stares me in the face,

This unimpeded sun!—
And for my hand,
The fine unfecund yellow sand!

DUET

(I sing with myself)

Out of my sorrow
I'll build a stair,
And every tomorrow
Will climb to me there—

With ashes of yesterday
In its hair.

My fortune is made
Of a stab in the side,
My debts are paid
In pennies of pride—

Little red coins
In a heart I hide.

The stones that I eat
Are ripe for my needs,
My cup is complete
With the dregs of deeds—

Clear are the notes
Of my broken reeds.

I carry my pack
Of aches and stings,
Light with the lack
Of all good things—

But not on my back,
Because of my wings!

NEW ENGLAND COTTAGE

The house is all in wooden rags,
The chimney tilts, the gable sags,
And where I pass
Are weedy flags
That my feet guess.

A horse-shoe rusts above the door,
Young roses prowl the porch's floor,
Up in the dark
Wide sycamore
Is thrushes' talk.

And here, a well not yet gone dry!
Lean in and meet its mellow eye,
Look deep, to where
A round of sky
Lurks with its star.

Happy old house of moldy beams,
Of cobweb rooms and loosening seams,
Besieged old walls
That guard their dreams
Like sentinels.

Old ark—slow-withering stick and stone,
Oak flesh that fades on iron bone;
And not deserted,
Just alone
And drowsy-hearted.

Let not my death be long,
But light
As a bird's swinging;
Happy decision in the height
Of song—
Then flight
From off the ultimate bough!
And let my wing be strong,
And my last note the first
Of another's singing.
See to it, Thou!

Mark Van Doren

SPRING THUNDER

Listen. The wind is still,
And far away in the night—
See! The uplands fill
With a running light.

Open the doors. It is warm;
And where the sky was clear—
Look! The head of a storm
That marches here!

Come under the trembling hedge—
Fast, although you fumble.
There! Did you hear the edge
Of winter crumble?

BOY DRESSING

There lies the shoe, picked up a minute past
And dropped when something struck him, and he
           paused,
Eye-rigid, fixing daylight on the door:
Thin daylight, that a careless clock has caused

And windows have conspired with. So his hands,
Conscious of nothing leather, float to work
At buttons on his breast, and at the tie—
He fumbles round it; finishes with a jerk;

Stops dead again, his hair in timeless tangles,
Obedient to a moment that will end—
Bang! Doors downstairs have doomed it. But the
           shoe
Remembering, his back begins to bend,

His knee comes up, his fingers at the instep
Play with the knotted laces. Leave him there.
Be tolerant of trances. For he feeds
On time, and drinks the milk of mother air.

AFTERWARDS

The stalls were empty in the shed;
    Nothing grazed beyond the gate.
But there was straw to make a bed,
    And the four bridles dangled straight.

We heard the water running cold,
    As she had left it, round the crocks.
Linen lay for us to fold
    And there was pepper in the box.

The very trap that she had set
    To catch a mole that loved the lawn
Hung above the passage yet;
    Another mole was boring on.

The wounded deer still fled the dog
    Within the gold and walnut frame;
The Fishermen Among the Fog,
    And The Young Mother, were the same.

We laughed to see a boot behind
    The stove; but then you wept
At your happening to find
    Spectacles where she had slept.

Audrey Wurdemann

ONLY THE BLACKBIRD

Only the blackbird will insist
On his one note; the thrush
Rummages like a botanist
And the bee burrs in plush
While that sweet ventriloquist
The cuckoo, cannot hush.

And this is well, and that is well,
And summer has no use for death.
The snail coiled in his thrice-coiled shell
Partakes one little smoky breath
Before the frost invokes that spell
That ends in winter's shibboleth.

Only the blackbird: all the rest
Are singing a hundred songs of fire
To ward away the winter lest
It feed on them and their desire;

Only the blackbird whistles well
His one clear note; only the snail
Leaves one unsteady silver trail;
Only are left, when the frost is over,
Lost in the roots of the dying clover,
A red-tipped feather, a red-lipped shell.

SPRING SONG

The sweet wild dogwood wears its flowers
Through silent shadow-patterned hours,
And ivory creamcups make a star
Where robins and wake-robin are.
The Judas trees let crimson drip
From each spire-pointed finger tip,
And bishop's croziers unfold
To dust the ginger-root with gold.
Then, gathering all her loveliness,
Spring goes, and leaves us no address.

THE WEAVERS

With web on ceiling and web on wall,
The shawls of the weavers shadow the hall,
And the weavers people the quiet spaces.
From door ajar to the lintel bar,
And back again to the hinge, the traces
Of corded silk make a woven star.
Thin-shinned those olden spinners are,
All squat from sitting at the loom;
And, in the twilight, or the gloom
Of rain without, if one brought light
To live in that too-silent spot,
The spinners' eyes would glow as hot
As red-rimmed coals, with little sight
From peering long at webs pulled tight.
And if anyone should call and call,
The weavers would not speak at all
As men, but from those pendent thrones
Would sound the crack of knucklebones.

TARTARY

Under the shards of shattered stone
The bells are mute, nor has anyone
For centuries shaken, petal by petal,
The songs that ring through stricken metal;
Nor anyone stirred the blood poured in
When the molten bronze ran ruddy thin;
And none has called to the living voice,
And heard it, answering, rejoice.
This is the fate of a buried bell
With all the tales of the khans to tell.
There shall be only ghosts to listen
Deep in the dust where nothing can glisten,
And a pebble as bright as a diamond or two
Lost from a Mongol emperor's shoe.
There shall be only a silence deeper
Than any quiet about a sleeper,
And the quick-eyed mice with fur-like rust
Shall leave their prints in gathering dust.

Marya Zaturenska

THE DAISY

Having so rich a treasury, so fine a hoard
Of beauty water-bright before my eyes,
I plucked the daisy only, simple and white
In its fringed frock and brooch of innocent gold.

So is all equilibrium restored:
I leave the noontide wealth of richer bloom
To the destroyer, the impatient ravisher,
The intemperate bee, the immoderate bird.

Of all this beauty felt and seen and heard,
I can be frugal and devout and plain,
Deprived so long of light and air and grass,
The shyest flower is sweetest to uncover.

How poor I was: and yet no richer lover
Discovered joy so deep in earth and water;
And in the air that fades from blue to pearl,
And in a flower white-frocked like my small
            daughter.

RENEWAL OF FOUNTAINS

Bright universe unseen, yet seen awhile,
Precious and brief in a tree bathed in light
And in shy, sudden flowers,
In rain, in hasty storm.

Or where the air is moist with trancèd heat
Under the noonday sun remote and high
We wander and are lost
In golden-shadowy lanes.

Or in the hyacinth shadows of the night
Where the black hills' immaculate, warm line
Meets with translucent blue
And the dark waters run.

With silver-pointed stars for company,
Light-tipped, soft-shaded, deep, the world
        revolves
To eloquent bright eyes
That pierce through shade.

All this endures, revives and calms the mind
When the harsh day is done, the bitter wars

And winter's icy voice
Chills sky and air.

Here, waiting for renewal, fountains play,
Sparkling, inviting, dancing and withdrawn
Hope withers and is green,
Destroyed, restored.

Wanderer in intricate paths, bewildered soul,
When all that pleased you once shall please no
             more,
Rest and desire no rest
Under the common grass.

LULLABY

Ruin falls on blackening skies
And disaster lies in wait
For the heart and for the state,
Loud the voices in the street
Shout unhealing remedies.

Sleep, beloved, while you may:
Heralds of the Augustan day
That arise as you awake
Can consume but never slake
The strong thirst, intense and deep,
For the peace that need not sleep.

Let the lion have his hour,
Let the evil beasts devour
Leaf and vine and fruit and flower,
Theirs the night but yours the time
Known to the Vergilian rhyme
When the ancient world, distressed,
Found peace in an infant's breast.

Still remote and gay and young
Sing the stars in ancient peace,

Heralding the great release
In their wordless tongue.
Close your eyes and let them sing
In the morning that will bring
What strange beasts to haunt the spheres?
Revelations? New-found fears?

Let the old world fall away
As the great beasts leave their prey;
Let the dogs and cats destroy
That which they cannot enjoy.
New as life and death and sleep
Shall the cyclic rivers creep,
Bringing learning, art and thought
New again to be renewed,
Revived, restored, and still uncaught,
The intangible pursued.

Sleep, beloved, in the changes
Light from bright to darkness ranges:
Venus, ocean-young, arises,
Love again the earth surprises
Naked, dreaming, peaceful, free,
Springing from the bitter sea
Of unending destiny.

About the Poets

ABOUT THE POETS*

CONRAD AIKEN (Born in Savannah, Georgia, in 1889)

When he was twelve years old, Conrad Aiken, who was to become one of the most original and foremost of modern American poets, wrote a poem which began with the lines

Hid in the tangles of grass all day
The lion crouches in wait for his prey.

---

* For critical quotations appearing in the following brief biographies, the compiler wishes to acknowledge the following sources:

The Boston Transcript, The Chicago Daily News, The Christian Science Monitor, The New York Herald-Tribune, The New York Times, The Atlantic Monthly, The Bookman, Esquire, The Nation, The New Republic, Outlook, Poetry: A Magazine of Verse, The Saturday Review of Literature, Scholastic, The Spokesman, Time, and *The Yale Review.*

For various additional quotations the compiler wishes to express her appreciation also to the following publishers:

Richard Blank, Inc.; Duffield and Green, Inc.; E. P. Dutton and Company; Farrar and Rinehart, Inc.; Harcourt, Brace and Company; Henry Holt and Company; Houghton Mifflin Company; B. W. Heubsch, Inc.; The Macmillan Company; The A. N. Marquis Company; Random House, Inc.; Charles Scribner's Sons; and the H. W. Wilson Company.

For this poem his school gave him a gold medal with his name engraved on it. He resolved to be a poet.

Both his father and mother had tragic, sudden deaths shortly after this, and he was taken to New Bedford, Massachusetts, where he lived with his great-great aunt and had a room like a small lookout tower, facing the sea and the fishing smacks in the harbor. Here young Conrad read Poe's poems and reveled in "The City in the Sea."

He was still writing poems when he went to Harvard, and college publications printed them. One poem took him ten days to do. The authorities objected to his cutting classes (where his standing was high) for those ten days. The poet, provoked, left college for six months and spent the time traveling in Italy. Later he returned to Harvard and was class poet in 1911, in a college generation that included Van Wyck Brooks, Walter Lippmann, T. S. Eliot, the late Alan Seeger, John Reed, and Heywood Broun.

Since he had an independent income, he never felt it necessary to write merely for money. He traveled widely, but continued to come back to Cambridge. He published sixteen books of verse, a number of anthologies, some short stories and novels, and many criticisms. Once he wrote a ruthless, anonymous review of his book *Nocturne of Remembered Spring*, exposing his own literary faults. Once he brought out an English edition of *Selected Poems of Emily Dickinson*, whose work he says is "perhaps the finest by a woman in the English language."

In 1930 he took his second wife and his three children to England, where he bought a house in Rye, Sussex, which in October 1940 narrowly escaped a bomb. While there he wrote, under a pseudonym, the "London Letter" for *The New Yorker*.

He has returned to America and is now with his third wife, the artist Mary Hoover Aiken, "the proud possessor of an eight-acre plantation of poison ivy in the midmost jungle of Cape Cod."

Mr. Aiken has been made the central subject of a work on modern poetry, *The Melody of Chaos*, by Houston Peterson.

His books are: *Earth Triumphant* (1914), *Turns and Movies* (1916), *The Jig of Forslin* (1916), *Nocturne of Remembered Spring* (1917), *The Charnel Rose* (1918), *Scepticisms—Notes on Contemporary Poetry* (1919), *The House of Dust* (1920), *Punch, the Immortal Liar* (1921), *Priapus and the Pool* (1922), *Modern American Poets* (1922; an anthology), *Pilgrimage of Festus* (1923), *Selected Poems of Emily Dickinson* (1924; editor), *Priapus and the Pool and Other Poems* (1925), *Bring! Bring!* (1925; short stories), *Blue Voyage* (1927; a novel), *Costumes by Eros* (1928; short stories), *Selected Poems* (1929; Pulitzer Prize-winning volume, 1930), *American Poetry, 1671-1928* (1929; an anthology), *John Deth and Other Poems* (1930), *The Coming Forth by Day of Osiris Jones* (1931), *Preludes to Memnon* (1931), *Great Circle* (1933; a novel), *Among the Lost People* (1934; short stories), *Landscape West of Eden* (1934; poems), *King Coffin* (1935; a novel), *Time in the Rock* (1936; poems), *A Heart for the Gods of Mexico* (1939; a novel), *The Conversation* (1939; a novel), and *And in the Human Heart* (1940).

Aiken says of his own poetry:

Here I give myself away as being in quest of a sort of absolute poetry, a poetry in which the intention is not so much to arouse an emotion, or to persuade of a reality, as to employ such emotion or sense of reality (tangentially struck) with the same cool detachment with which a composer employs notes or chords.

[169]

Tributes to Conrad Aiken:

> Conrad Aiken is one of the finest verbal musicians in this country; his work is rich in color and incident, thoughtful without losing itself in the jungles of the mind, distinguished without being flagrantly bizarre. . . . With a fresh point of departure and a genuine adjustment to the world of reality, Aiken may find a larger power and a wider audience. And whether the medium be prose or verse, his sensitivity need not be lost; it may well add new values to the roaring diapason of our day.
>
> —LOUIS UNTERMEYER
>
> Conrad Aiken has a rare, imaginative quality that seems to delight in the unexpected association of incongruous ideas.
>
> —JOHN LEWIS HANEY
>
> His poetry is best known for its beautiful musical cadence. It is the finest poetry written by a Southern poet since Poe.
>
> —ALAN RAMSAY

LEONARD BACON (Born at Solvay, New York, in 1887)

When Leonard Bacon entered Yale University, there were five members of his family on the faculty. In fact, members of both his father's and his mother's families had long been identified with that institution.

Mr. Bacon, his education interrupted by frequent journeys in search of health, was graduated from Yale in 1909. A year later he was living up to the family tradition and teaching freshman English at the University of California. Later he was to become an assistant professor on the same faculty. For the last years of the war, he served as a second lieutenant in the United States Air Service.

Although he had been writing poetry all his life, he did not start publishing it until 1923, and from that

[170]

time on gave up teaching and devoted his entire time to writing. He is married and has three daughters. His home now is at Peace Dale, Rhode Island.

His books are: *Ulug Beg* (1923), *PhDs* (1925), *Animula Vagula* (1926), *Guinea Fowl and Other Poultry* (1927), *The Legend of Quincibald* (1928), *Lost Buffalo* (1930), *The Furiosa* (1932). Translator: (with G. R. Noyes) *Heroic Ballads of Servia* (1913), *The Song of Roland* (1914); (with R. Selden Rose) *The Lay of the Cid* (1919), *Dream of Action* (1934), *The Voyage of Autoleon* (1935), *The Goose on the Capitol* (1936), *Rhyme and Punishment* (1936), *Bullinger Bound* (1938), *Semi-Centennial* (1939), *Sunderland Capture* (1940; Pulitzer Prize for 1941).

Leonard Bacon says of poetry:

It is a platitude to say that pleasure is what we ought to derive from poetry. . . . "It is the heat of the poet's feeling rather than his thought that matters." And that heat ought to bring out the human in whatever he touches.

Tributes to Leonard Bacon:

The wide range of his observation, [and] . . . his broad scholarship and spicy satire, are definite qualities of his verse, and always one can find a breath for beauty and the enduring realities.

—RALPH WENDELL

The author is a man who has dared to meet himself face to face. . . . Both [of his long poems in *Sunderland Capture*] are worth reading for the spiritual courage they show.

—BABETTE DEUTSCH

Leonard Bacon is prolific, vigorous, tender, satirical, sometimes even savage, but in spite of some good work he has done in the ballad (which takes energy) he is really one of the best satirists of our time.

—JOHN HOLMES

[171]

STEPHEN VINCENT BENÉT (Born in Bethlehem, Pennsylvania, in 1898)

Battles and Leaders, old *Army Records,* and the *Lives of the Roman Emperors* were among the first books to interest the author of that powerful Pulitzer Prize epic *John Brown's Body;* and in those early days, growing up in army posts all over the country, the young omnivorous reader listened eagerly when his father, Colonel James Walker Benét of the United States Army, recited such lines as Browning's

I sprang to the stirrup and Joris and he;
I galloped, Dirck galloped, we galloped all three.

For generations the Benéts had been military men, both in Spain (Minorca) and in America. Brigadier General Stephen Vincent Benét, the poet's grandfather, was Chief of Ordnance of the United States Army, and Chief Justice Holmes once said: "The first book I read by the bearer of this name was a *Treatise on Military Law;* the next, many years later, was an epic poem!"

Stephen Vincent Benét as well as his distinguished brother and sister, William Rose and Laura Benét, began to write at an early age. By the time he was twelve his verse was being published in the *St. Nicholas* League. At seventeen his book of excellent dramatic monologues, *Five Men and Pompey,* came out. While he was still in Yale, his second book was published. William Lyon Phelps, one of his teachers at Yale, described him as universally popular and a sparkling conversationalist. He was an associate editor of *Youth,* an intercollegiate poetry magazine "that died to make verse free," was chairman of the Yale Literary Magazine, won three poetry prizes, and counted among his Yale friends Philip Barry, Archibald MacLeish, and Thornton Wilder.

[172]

After graduating from Yale he tried advertising, wrote a novel, and took his M.A. Then he went to France and studied at the Sorbonne. He continued his writing, and a Guggenheim Fellowship in 1926 allowed him to go to France again and work for two years on *John Brown's Body*. Among his later works, built around American folklore, have been his *Headless Horseman,* an operetta on the radio; *The Devil and Daniel Webster,* his most famous story turned into an opera and performed in New York; and *Johnny Pye and the Fool Killer.* Aside from the Pulitzer Prize, he has won the *Nation's* poetry prize, the Roosevelt Medal for his contribution to American letters, and the Shelley Memorial Award. He is vice-president of the National Institute of Arts and Letters and the editor of the Yale Series of Younger Poets. He is said to be the original of Ben Vincent, a character in Cyril Hume's *The Wife of the Centaur,* written in 1923. He is married, has three children, and lives in New York.

His books are: *Five Men and Pompey* (1915), *Young Adventure* (1918), *Heavens and Earth* (1920), *The Beginning of Wisdom* (1921), *Jean Huguenot* (1923), *Tiger Joy* (1925), *Spanish Bayonet* (1926), *John Brown's Body* (1928; Pulitzer Prize in 1929), *Ballads and Poems* (1931), *James Shore's Daughter* (1934), *Burning City* (1936), *The Devil and Daniel Webster* (1937), *Thirteen O'Clock* (1937), *Johnny Pye and the Fool Killer* (1938), and *Tales Before Midnight* (1939).

Tributes to Stephen Vincent Benét:

John Brown's Body is poignantly and exhaustingly alive. . . . Its fusion of life, art, and critical acumen in flights of lyric poetry with final dramatic effect offers its audience, at one and the same time, a vivid vicarious experience and an

[173]

important philosophical comment. This may be high praise, but so it is.

—Hervey Allen

He writes it to please himself according to the demands of his own temperament. His mind is vigorous and intensely alive. Criticism he takes with a drawl and a twinkle. . . .

A good poet; a man of strong affection; a good man at a venture!

—William Rose Benét

His poetry is at times entirely compelling. It contains lines and passages that one would gladly remember forever. . . . It is sustained by a fine sincerity—by the poet's own heart honestly feeling all that is felt—and it is adorned with interruptions of excellent lyrical song.

—Max Eastman

Robert P. Tristram Coffin (Born in Brunswick, Maine, 1892)

"Any man who has a pair of good eyes and ears and a residence in the State of Maine," says Robert P. Tristram Coffin, "has a pretty fair equipment for setting up housekeeping as a poet."

Mr. Coffin has this equipment. Coming from an old family of Nantucket whalers, he was reared in Maine and educated there at Bowdoin, from which he was graduated in 1915 *summa cum laude*. Later he took an M.A. at Princeton, a B.A. at Oxford (where he was a Rhodes scholar), and a Litt.D. at the University of Maine. He taught English at Wells College, and, since 1934, has been professor of English at Bowdoin. In 1928 he was the Phi Beta Kappa poet at Harvard, and in 1936 he won the Pulitzer Prize for his book of verse *Strange Holiness*. He is married, has four children and two farms, and lives in Brunswick.

[174]

His books are: *Christchurch* (poems; 1924), *Book of Crowns and Cottages* (essays; 1925), *Dew and Bronze* (verse; 1927), *Golden Falcon* (verse; 1929), *An Attic Room* (essays; 1929), *Laud, Storm Center of Stuart England* (biography; 1930), *The Dukes of Buckingham* (1931), *Portrait of an American* (1931), *The Yoke of Thunder* (verse; 1932), *Ballads of Square-Toed Americans* (verse; 1933), *Lost Paradise* (autobiography; 1934), *Strange Holiness* (verse; 1935), *Red Sky in the Morning* (novel; 1935), *John Dawn* (novel; 1936), *Saltwater Farm* (verse; 1937), *Kennebec: Cradle of Americans* (Rivers of America series; historical; 1937), *New Poetry of New England* (Turnbull Lectures, Johns Hopkins University; 1938), *Maine Ballads* (verse; 1938), *Collected Poems* (1939), *Captain Abby and Captain John* (biography; 1939). Compiler: *A Book of Seventeenth Century Prose* (with A. M. Witherspoon; 1929).

Mr. Coffin says of poetry:

I have a feeling that poetry can still be a *public function*, as it once was. It can be *oratory* and can convince people of the possibility of design in living, and supply the pattern that once was inherent in religion but that religion is losing for many people today.

Poetry is saying the best one can about life. . . . Poetry is the best arrangement of the finest thoughts. . . . It is the art of making people feel well about life.

I have found poems in the light of common days, but I have found them also in a sudden radiance like that on the road to Damascus. . . . These are poems a poet does not have to write. They are poems that come to him, and he has only to set them down. One or two of them can make any man cling to the precious chance of being alive.

Tributes to Robert P. Tristram Coffin:

Robert Coffin, with his honest, homespun poetry, has woven something useful and noble into our national fabric. May his torch of native pine burn a long time.

—Percy Hutchison

Mr. Coffin soon came under the influence of Robert Frost,

[175]

who helped him to see the poetry in common speech and people and in everyday sights. He has written some quiet, unforgettable lyrics of great beauty.

—ALAN RAMSAY

Robert P. Tristram Coffin's collected volume contains some striking things. More sentimental than Mr. Van Doren, his poetry is also more highly colored, sometimes with fine pictorial effect. He knows New England farm life, loves the State of Maine, can paint a vivid portrait or crack the whip of a fine ballad measure. His fault is facility. . . . But he is an enjoyable American poet.

—WILLIAM ROSE BENÉT

GEORGE DILLON (Born in Jacksonville, Florida, in 1906)

One of the youngest poets to receive the Pulitzer Prize is George Dillon, who won several poetry prizes during his student days at the University of Chicago. Here he was the president of the famous University of Chicago Poetry Club (which included among its members such writers as Maurice Lesemann, Glenway Wescott, Elizabeth Madox Roberts, and Vincent Sheean). He founded the *Forge*, a magazine of verse, and for two years was associate editor of *Poetry*. He received the Pulitzer Prize for *The Flowering Stone* in 1932, when he was twenty-six years old, and also the Guggenheim Award, which allowed him to study two years in France.

George Dillon's childhood was spent in Florida, Kentucky, and Cincinnati, and before coming to Chicago he attended the School of Fine Arts in St. Louis. For three years after he was graduated from college, he wrote advertising copy. Then he turned again to writing and studying poetry. He admires contemporary verse dealing with social themes, and modern British poets, includ-

[176]

ing W. H. Auden and T. S. Eliot. At present he is editor of *Poetry Magazine,* and his home is in Richmond, Virginia.

His books are: *Boy in the Wind* (1927), *The Flowering Stone* (1931), and a translation (with Edna St. Vincent Millay) of *Flowers of Evil* from the French of Charles Baudelaire.

George Dillon once said of one of his poems:

The Noise of Leaves . . . comes nearer than anything else I have done to saying what cannot be said—in short, nearer to poetry.

Tributes to George Dillon:

These new poems confirm Dillon's place among the more distinguished of his fellows. There is evidence in this volume [*The Flowering Stone*] that he has been attentive to such lessons as they had to give him. But whatever he may have learned from his fellow-craftsmen, no poet save himself can have brought him to the source of his poetry or unsealed that bright fountain to our refreshment and joy. Only a searching mind and an alert, sensitive body could have combined to produce poetry of this calibre.

—BABETTE DEUTSCH

Refreshing and lovely, full of poignant beauty, entirely unstudied in expression.

—BERNICE KENYON

Here the ancient virtues of clarity and flexibility, freshness and sensitivity are still honored. . . . *The Flowering Stone* has moved in the direction of the impersonal and the philosophical, without losing the crystalline purity of the earlier volume.

—FRED B. MILLETT

JOHN GOULD FLETCHER (Born in Little Rock, Arkansas, in 1886)

The United States has something that is lacking in the decaying civilization of Europe, "a necessary resistance,

[177]

that fundamental give and take that is so essential to the arts."

This is the conviction reached by John Gould Fletcher, whose *Selected Poems* won the Pulitzer Prize in 1939. He, with T. S. Eliot and Ezra Pound, had belonged to an experimental group of expatriates who had felt Europe more hospitable than America to artists. For twenty years or more he had lived abroad and written much experimental free verse there. But since 1933 he has been living in America.

Mr. Fletcher had an Arkansas childhood. His father, a Confederate veteran, came from a family of Scotch-Irish pioneers. The poet studied at home with his mother, an accomplished and gifted woman of German and Danish extraction. He hated mathematics and loved history, "felt within the walls of his father's house the presence of the antebellum South which influenced him deeply," read Scott, Tennyson, Coleridge, Shakespeare, and the Bible. Then came school days at Andover and college days at Harvard, where he began to write poetry. He left before he was graduated. He thought he would like to be an archeologist; but when he went abroad he spent five years with his literary friends, reading the French Symbolists, writing much verse that he never published, and publishing, himself, one volume he never liked. He began to put his poems into free forms, "according to the state of his feelings and the condition of his material," and he began to write about "things that one can hear, see, smell or taste." Amy Lowell discovered this verse of his and persuaded him to appear in her famous and much-discussed anthology, *Some Imagists*. Since then he has written many books of poetry and of literary criticism as well as his autobiography. He received his LL.D. from the University of Arkansas in

1933 and the Pulitzer Prize for his *Selected Poems* in 1939.

He has been married twice, and now lives in Roland, Arkansas.

His books are: *Fire and Wine* (1913), *Fool's Gold* (1913), *The Dominant City* (1913), *The Book of Nature* (1913), *Visions of the Evening* (1913), *Irradiations, Sand and Spray* (1916), *Goblins and Pagodas* (1916), *Japanese Prints* (1918), *The Tree of Life* (1918), *Breakers and Granite* (1921), *Paul Gauguin, His Life and Art* (1921; a biography), *Preludes and Symphonies* (1922), *Parables* (1925), *Branches of Adam* (1926), *John Smith—Also Pocahontas* (1928), *The Black Rock* (1928), *The Two Frontiers* (1930), *XXIV Elegies* (1935), *The Epic of Arkansas* (1936), *Life Is My Song* (1937; autobiography), and *Selected Poems* (1938; Pulitzer Prize volume of 1939; translated, two volumes).

Fletcher says of literature:

I hold the chief function of literature to be the transposition of life into the medium of language, rather than any direct attempt to imitate life. I do not therefore regard very highly literature that aims at realism—I prefer fantasy and imagination to exact documentation. Literature should interpret and order the facts of life; and the interpretation I try to present is always colored by the imagination. In short, I suppose you would call me a romantic, insofar as I rate the sensibility of the author as being of equal importance with the material with which he deals. I also question the social importance of literature—it seems to me a matter of individual taste.

Tributes to John Gould Fletcher:

He calls himself an advanced liberal and can find no place in the land for fascism or communism. Free speech and freest expression must be maintained. Only the élite can save the world and develop a greater race.

—ALFRED KREYMBORG

[179]

The sort of poet who reaches his greatest brilliance when allowed to develop rapidly successive musical variations on a theme capable of prolonged treatment.

—Conrad Aiken

He has achieved much in descriptive poetry, and his later work has borne deep philosophic content.

—William Rose Benét

Robert Frost (Born in San Francisco, California, in 1875)

Although Robert Lee Frost is a ninth-generation New Englander, he was actually born in San Francisco, where his father was in politics. His father was a Yankee with Southern sympathies, and named his son after General Lee.

Mr. Frost's mother, a schoolteacher, moved back to New England after her husband's death. A passage in Vergil's *Georgics* in a Lawrence, Massachusetts, high school made her son understand what it was to be a poet, and he began to write. He left Dartmouth, which seemed too academic for him, and started working as a bobbin boy in a Lawrence mill. He married at the age of twenty, later spent two years at Harvard, then left and began to teach. After this he made shoes, edited the Lawrence *Sentinel,* and became a farmer. When the farm failed, Mr. and Mrs. Frost sailed for England, where they lived in a thatched cottage in Beaconsfield, and where Robert Frost continued to write poetry. He presently published his first two books, *A Boy's Will* and *North of Boston,* which achieved much success in England and later in America.

When the poet returned to America in 1915, he found himself famous. Since then he has been Poet in Residence at Amherst, the University of Michigan, and Harvard, where he is now the Charles Eliot Norton Professor of Poetry.

His fine verse about New England has won him many honors, including the Pulitzer Prize for poetry in 1924, 1931, and 1937, for *New Hampshire, Collected Poems,* and *A Further Range,* and honorary degrees from thirteen colleges. His friends speak of him as a quiet, kind, keen, and friendly man who takes long walks and nearly always carries a book with him, a wholesome philosopher who writes when he feels like it—usually very late at night.

His books are: *A Boy's Will* (1913), *North of Boston* (1914), *Mountain Interval* (1916), *New Hampshire* (1923), *West-running Brook* (1928), *A Way Out* (1929; a play), *Selected Poems* (1923 and 1928), *Collected Poems* (1930), *A Lone Striker* (1933), *A Further Range* (1936), and *From Snow to Snow* (1936).

Robert Frost's definition of a poem:

A poem begins with a lump in the throat; a homesickness or a love-sickness. It is a reaching out towards expression; an effort to find fulfillment. A complete poem is one where an emotion has found its thought and the thought has found the words.

Tributes to Mr. Frost:

The poetic feeling for ordinary life is expressed . . . so simply and yet so richly in the work of Robert Frost. The mending of a wall, the gathering of blueberries, a patch of old snow, a cow in apple-time, a dried-up brook, two people moving into a new house, a couple coming home to an old one—these things are used not as decorations or themes for moral embroidery, or incidents to be lifted to a "poetic" plane, but as pictures and happenings intrinsically beautiful,

[181]

to be enjoyed not for their possibilities but for themselves. . . .

He has given emotion, thought and words such national flavor and freshness that no poet since Whitman has been more American and, in his very localism, more universal.

—Louis Untermeyer

Nowhere else can we find in all its pungency that piquant, aromatic raciness which is New England.

—T. K. Whipple

Mr. Frost writes down *exactly* what he sees. But, being a true poet, he says it vividly and with a charm which translates itself into a beautiful simplicity of expression. He is an eminently sympathetic poet. He wins first by his gentle understanding, and his strong and unsentimental power of emotion; later, we are conquered by his force, and moved to admiration by his almost unapproachable technique. Still, his imagination is bounded by his life, he is confined within the limits of his experience (or at least what might have been his experience) and bent all one way like the wind-blown trees of New England hillsides. After all, art is rooted in the soil, and only the very greatest men can be both cosmopolitan and great. Mr. Frost is as New England as Burns is Scotch, Synge Irish, or Mistral Provençal, and it is perhaps not too much to say that he is the equal of these poets, and will so rank to future generations.

—Amy Lowell

ROBERT HILLYER (Born in East Orange, New Jersey, in 1895)

Freed of all obligation to enlist
On any side, triumphant Quietist.

At least one critic said that Robert Hillyer, Harvard professor, Phi Beta Kappa poet, and winner of the Pulitzer Prize, was describing himself when he wrote these

[182]

lines. He, too, is a "triumphant Quietist," who does not care to write about the events of our time.

Mr. Hillyer, who writes music as well as poetry of great artistic restraint, and who greatly admires the work of Robert Bridges, divides his time between teaching English at Harvard and seclusion at Pomfret, Connecticut.

During his college days at Harvard he won a poetry prize. During the First World War he was an ambulance driver in the French Army, and later a first lieutenant with the American Expeditionary Force. Immediately after the war he acted as a courier for the Peace Conference. Since 1920, however, he has taught English, first at Trinity College in Connecticut and later at Harvard, where he now occupies the Boylston Chair of Rhetoric and Oratory—a chair formerly occupied by Charles Townsend Copeland and before him by a line of worthies ranging from John Quincy Adams to Dean L. B. R. Briggs. He was away one year, during which he held a fellowship of the American-Scandinavian Foundation and studied at the University of Copenhagen.

For two years Mr. Hillyer was president of the New England Poetry Society. He received an honorary master's degree at Trinity. He has been Phi Beta Kappa poet at Harvard, at Columbia, and at the College of William and Mary. He is a fellow of the American Academy of Arts and Sciences and a member of the National Institute of Arts and Letters. His *Collected Verse* won the Pulitzer Prize in 1934. He is married and has one son.

His books are: *Eight Harvard Poets* (1917), *Sonnets and Other Lyrics* (1917), *Alchemy, a Symphonic Poem* (1920), *The Five Books of Youth* (1920), *The Hills Give Promise* (1923), *The Coming Forth By Day* (1923), *The Halt in the Garden* (1925), *The Happy Episode* (1927), *The Engage-*

[183]

ment Ring (a play; 1927), *The Masquerade* (a play; 1928), *The Seventh Hill* (1928), *The Gates of the Compass and Other Poems* (1930), *Riverhead* (a novel; 1932), *Collected Verse* (1933), *Some Roots of English Poetry* (1933), *A Letter to Robert Frost and Others* (1937), *First Principles of Verse* (1938), *In Time of Mistrust* (1939), and *Pattern of a Day* (1940).

Tributes to Robert Hillyer:

He has followed the old tradition with technical skill and polish. . . . Classical influences are evident in his work, which combines richness of imagery with a distinctive serenity in spirit.

—John Lewis Haney

He is an excellent technician. He never blurs a form or overemphasizes an image.

—*The Nation*

Amy Lowell (Born in Brookline, Massachusetts, in 1874; died in 1925)

"The High Priestess of *Vers Libre*," as Miss Lowell has been called, was one of America's most brilliant and original poets. She came from a distinguished New England family. Her grandfather's cousin was James Russell Lowell. Her father was the head of Lowell Institute. Her two brothers were Percival Lowell, the astronomer who charted the canals of Mars, and Abbott Lawrence Lowell, President Emeritus of Harvard.

Amy Lowell's energetic childhood and most of her busy life were spent in "Sevenels," the family home in Brookline. In this large, slate-roofed brick house, five miles from the center of Boston, Miss Lowell studied French and music with her mother, read books omnivorously, and did a little writing. Outside, amid the ten

[184]

acres of the old-fashioned gardens, lawns, graveled paths, groves of trees, and rolling meadows, she flew kites, rolled hoops, played tennis, rode horseback, and reveled in her gardening. She continued her studies with private tutors and at boarding school. Then, when she was twenty-one, her mother died and she took her second voyage abroad. A serious illness interrupted a trip on the Nile. For the next few years she traveled extensively in Greece, Turkey, England, and many other foreign countries.

At twenty-eight Miss Lowell decided to be a poet, and spent much time in learning her craft. The *Atlantic* published her first poem in 1910, and two years later her first book appeared. In England she met Ezra Pound, H.D., Richard Aldington, and John Gould Fletcher. Soon she had become the leader of their Imagist Group, turning away from all abstractions and expressing herself vividly as a modern. Miss Lowell now took up the cudgels for polyphonic prose, "using the many voices of poetry, *vers libre,* meter, assonance, alliteration, rhyme and return. Polyphonic prose employs every form of rhythm, even prose rhythm at times." She was a vigorous champion and leader of the new poetry. Over and over again she declared that each poet should have the right to express himself as he wished. Over and over again she said this from lecture platforms and from the pages of magazines and newspapers.

Miss Lowell was kind, shrewd, fastidious, witty, domineering, and delightful. As her books increased her reputation, her odd ways soon became widely known. The public remembered her as a stout, eccentric lady in a high-necked, black satin dress, a lady who smoked black cigars, wrote all night in her attic room and covered her mirror with black draperies; a lady who was followed by seven sheep dogs, who had all clocks stopped, who read in bed amid sixteen pillows, holding up a black umbrella in the bright light of mid-afternoon.

Miss Lowell identified herself with the cultural life of her city, lectured at Yale and Brown Universities, was twice a Phi Beta Kappa poet, and received her honorary Litt.D. from Tufts, Baylor, and Columbia Universities. Her last years were devoted to her scholarly life of Keats, in which she embodied her views on poetry. She died from overwork and a paralytic stroke in 1925. Her book of poems *What's O'Clock* won the Pulitzer Prize posthumously the following year. Two other books were published after her death. She bequeathed her manuscripts and her valuable collection of ten thousand books to Harvard, and provided for an Amy Lowell Poetry Traveling Scholarship, "to give each year to some poet of American birth, of good standing, of promise, two thousand dollars for a year's traveling, necessarily outside of North America."

Her books are: *A Dome of Many-Coloured Glass* (1912), *Sword Blades and Poppy Seeds* (1914), *Men, Women and Ghosts* (1916), *Can Grande's Castle* (1918), *Pictures of the Floating World* (1919), *Legends* (1921), *Fir-flower Tablets* (translated from the Chinese by Florence Ayscough; English versions by Amy Lowell; 1921), *What's O'Clock* (1925), *East Wind* (1926), *Ballads for Sale* (1927). Three of her prose volumes are: *Six French Poets* (1915), *Tendencies in Modern Poetry* (1917), and *John Keats* (1925).

Miss Lowell said of poetry:

I wish to state my firm belief that poetry should not try to teach, that it should exist simply because it is a creative beauty, even if sometimes the beauty of a Gothic grotesque.

Poetry, far more than fiction, reveals the soul of humanity. Poets are always the advance guard of literature; the advance

[186]

guard of life. It is for this reason that their recognition comes
so slowly.

Tributes to Amy Lowell:

If there is in America one poet more than another whose
name is a challenge, that poet is Miss Amy Lowell. She is
the propagandist of innovation. She is, besides, a most abun-
dant writer, and again and again she makes in unrhymed
and freely-rhymed verse poems that are undeniably beautiful.
. . . Not only is she a poet of distinction but she is a liberat-
ing influence on American poetry.

—PADRAIC COLUM

A consideration of her volumes must make it plain that
Miss Lowell's range is the most obvious of her gifts. But it
is not the greatest. She strikes single notes as sharply as she
sounds experimental chords. When her completed works are
some day appraised in a detailed study of American poetry,
it will be found that her versatile energies have expressed a
poet who is half-singer, half-scientist, and the groping, experimental period she helped represent.

—LOUIS UNTERMEYER

Inheritance, New England tradition demanded from Amy
Lowell a fixed conduct of life. . . . But the strength of her
individuality was too great to be anything but independent.
The conflict between the two forces drove the poet within
herself and caused her to create an ideal world of dreams.

—RICA BRENNER

The power of moving my strongest emotions is not in
Miss Lowell's poetry; the power of delighting my senses and
my intellect is always there. . . . She is one of our major
poets, beyond any question. . . . "Patterns" will certainly
remain one of the most remarkable in our poetry.

—WILLIAM ROSE BENÉT

ARCHIBALD MacLEISH (Born in Glencoe, Illinois, in 1892)

The Librarian of the Library of Congress, who has
written several anti-Fascist radio plays—a poet's means

[187]

of reaching a great audience—is the Pulitzer poet of 1933. Archibald MacLeish is not only a poet, a playwright, and a librarian; he has been a teacher, a lawyer, and an editor, and was a captain in the Army during the World War. His father, a Scot, was one of the early settlers of Chicago, a merchant who, the poet himself says, was "a cold, tall, rigorous man of very beautiful speech." His mother, a teacher at Vassar, came of "a seafaring family from the Connecticut coast, very passionate people with many mad among them: she was my father's third wife, intelligent and energetic and tireless and virtuous."

After four years in a fashionable Connecticut preparatory school, which he hated, Mr. MacLeish went to Yale, where he played football, was on the swimming team, was chairman of the *Literary Magazine*, and won his Phi Beta Kappa key. He led his class the last year at Harvard Law School, and after service in the war taught a year at Harvard and practiced law three years in Boston. Then, in the fall of 1923, with his wife and two children he went to France. For five years he traveled, read French poetry, and wrote English verse. On coming back home, he settled in Farmington, Connecticut, and served for a time on the editorial board of *Fortune Magazine*.

In the spring of 1929 he traveled alone in Mexico, going over the route of Cortez from San Juan de Ulua to Tenochtitlan and gathering background for his book *Conquistador*, which in 1933 won the Pulitzer Prize.

In the spring of 1939 he was appointed librarian of the Library of Congress.

One critic describes him thus:

Independent, courageous, he is not easily influenced; as a man of great personal charm and conviction, he often influences others. His manner is quiet, forthright, wholly without pose or affectation. His voice, his quick, boyish grin, his crisp hair that shows little gray make him look much too young to have grown-up sons.

The MacLeishes have varied friends and interests, but like to spend much time on their farm near Conway, Massachusetts.

His books are: *The Happy Marriage* (1924), *The Pot of Earth* (1925), *Nobodaddy* (verse play; 1925), *Streets in the Moon* (1926), *The Hamlet of A. MacLeish* (1928), *New Found Land* (1930), *Conquistador* (1932), *Frescoes for Mr. Rockefeller's City* (1933), *Union Pacific—A Ballet* (1934), *Panic* (verse play; 1935), *Public Speech* (verse; 1936), *The Fall of the City* (verse play for radio; 1937), *Land of the Free* (1938), *Air Raid* (verse play for radio; 1938), *America Was Promises* (1940).

Archibald MacLeish says of poetry:

There are no *a priori* rules about subject matter in verse, and the man who contends that there are is either an academician or that equally unimportant American phenomenon, the revolutionary pedant.

In that great unfinished definition of poetry in which Aristotle distinguished poetry from history he said: history draws things which have happened but poetry things which may possibly happen. In that word "possibly" is the whole aesthetic to justify the human and world-walking poetry of this generation. For the possibility of which Aristotle speaks is human possibility. History draws things which have happened; poetry things which are possible to men. In this time in which everything is possible except the spirit to desire and the love to choose, poetry becomes again the one deliverer of the people.

Tributes to Archibald MacLeish:

I am not sure what an authentic poet is, but I know Archibald MacLeish is one.

—CARL SANDBURG

Conquistador is one of the great tales of the world presented as if it came today from the mouth of a living man. . . . A magnificent and sustained achievement—solid with the solidity of good workmanship and informed with a masculine power and lyricism very rare at any time.

—STEPHEN VINCENT BENÉT

The felicity of cadence, the peculiar and resourceful faculty for translating native beauty . . . has marked all his work. . . . The man whose work has followed, as notes on a margin, the course of the major poetic attempts of his time, has at last apparently found root and inspiration in the vital contemporary struggle of the common man.

JOHN MALCOLM BRINNIN

EDNA ST. VINCENT MILLAY (Born in Rockland, Maine, in 1892)

"America has just two great works of art to its credit," said Thomas Hardy; "recessive architecture and the poetry of Edna St. Vincent Millay."

America's most famous lyric poet developed an amazing ability to write while still very young. She wrote poems, during her tomboy days in Rockland, for *St. Nicholas*. She won a prize for a high-school essay in verse, and a friend, impressed by her promise, helped her to go to college. At Vassar she was a shining literary light. She wrote plays and acted in them; she won an intercollegiate poetry contest. At nineteen she published "Renascence" in *The Lyric Year*. It was called, by many, one of the most brilliant poems of this generation.

After college came days in Greenwich Village. Here Miss Millay wrote poetry and poetic plays, acted for the Provincetown Players and for the Theater Guild, and published short stories under the pseudonym of Nancy Boyd. Some of her dramatic experiments were performed by Vassar students and by the Provincetown Players. Alfred Kreymborg recalls how she used to appear at rehearsals in these days: "When she appeared at all, an hour or two in arrears, her complete understanding of the pantomimic demands of her part compensated for her irregularity."

In 1923 she was awarded the Pulitzer Prize for Poetry for *The Harp-Weaver* and also for her volume *A Few Figs from Thistles*, which had been reprinted the preceding year. Some of Miss Millay's best sonnets are found in *The Harp-Weaver*.

The same year she was awarded the prize, she married Eugene Jan Boissevain, an importer, and they moved to a farm in the Berkshires. Since then she has had various homes in the Hudson Valley in New York State and on her own island off the Maine coast. She is fond of traveling abroad. Despite ill health, in 1927 Miss Millay did the libretto for an opera, *The King's Henchman,* the music for which was composed by Deems Taylor, and which was produced at the Metropolitan Opera House.

Miss Millay from time to time does a good deal of lecturing and recites her own poems "in a clear but excitingly husky voice." Llewelyn Powys once described her:

> She possessed the same fragile appearance, the same brittle, shell-like, pearl-like appearance that has always set me marveling. And her lovely leprechaun eyes, yellow-green in color, had the same strange light in them that I had observed at first, like . . . the eyes of an infinitely desirable mermaiden who finds a crowd of alien creatures looking down at her.

Other writers speak of her thick, coppery-gold hair, which was red in her childhood, of her poise, of her vivacity, and of the marked precision of her speech.

When she is in the mood for it, she works hard at her poetry. She thinks Robinson Jeffers is the greatest American poet.

Her books are: *Renascence and Other Poems* (1917), *A Few Figs from Thistles* (1920), *Second April* (1921), *Aria da Capo* (1921; a play), *The Lamp and the Bell* (1921; a play), *Two Slatterns and a King* (1921; a play), *The Harp-Weaver and Other Poems* (1923), *The King's Henchman* (1927), *The Buck in the Snow* (1928), *Selected Poems for Young People* (1929), *Fatal Interview* (1931), *Wine from These Grapes* (1934), *Flowers of Evil* (from the French of Charles Baudelaire, in collaboration with George Dillon; 1936), *Conversation at Midnight* (1937), and *Huntsman, What Quarry?* (1939).

Tributes to Edna St. Vincent Millay:

Miss Millay's lyrical gift is rare, her expression direct, her gift of irony unusual in a woman.

Her best work touches perfection. . . . She brings to the use of language that innate devotion which alone makes the superior poet. She is pre-eminent today as the finest living lyric poet among women in America.

—WILLIAM ROSE BENÉT

Everyone agrees that Miss Millay's best volumes of lyrics are *Renascence, Second April* and *Fatal Inverview.* While her early poetry expressed her hunger for beauty, was gay, frivolous, searching, her more recent verse has shown sadness, disillusion. In this she speaks up against cruelty and injustice. She was greatly stirred by the sights in Spain during the revolution, and her "Epitaph for the Race of Man" shows her realization of "the horrible and cruel things men do to each other." Miss Millay and Poe are the only American poets translated into Spanish.

—LLOYD A. JAMES

Hers is a voice that is both intellectually thrilling and emotionally moving.

—LOUIS UNTERMEYER

Fifty-two sonnets as fine as any in our language, and I am not forgetting anyone from Milton down to our own day.

Each sonnet stands alone in its austere beauty and greatness.
—CHARLES HANSON TOWNE

She is like nothing at all but herself; when she and this generation are gone, the die which stamped her style will be broken.

—ELINOR WYLIE

EDWIN ARLINGTON ROBINSON (Born in Head Tide, Maine, in 1869; died in 1935)

Three times winner of the Pulitzer Prize, and "the Father of Modern American poetry," Edwin Arlington Robinson once lived in New York "in a sordid stall on the fifth floor of a dreary house," and from his poetry for a long time "never made more than one hundred dollars a year."

The poet was brought up in Gardiner, Maine, the folksy Tilbury Town of his poems, and he came back there, after two years of Harvard, when the family fortune dwindled. In 1896 he brought out a small booklet of poems, *The Torrent and the Night Before*. A year later *The Children of the Night* was published.

Not long after this, Robinson was in New York working as a subway inspector when President Theodore Roosevelt wrote admiringly of his poems in *The Outlook*, hunted him up, and appointed him clerk in the New York Customs House. Later Robinson gave up this position in order to write. For the next eleven years he never made more than one hundred dollars a year out of his poetry. One day, in 1914, he had no money for breakfast. On that day the mail arrived, bringing him a letter telling that an old friend had left him four thousand dollars. "On this," said Robinson, "I thought I could live a million years."

Later on times grew better; the public began to recognize a real poet. He kept on writing, living simply in Boston and in New York during the winters and at the MacDowell Colony in Peterboro, New Hampshire, during the summers. His friends spoke of him as a grave, modest, scholarly man, a kindly fatalist, a shy and gentle agnostic. He loved detective stories, Dickens, *Moby Dick*, and Gilbert and Sullivan.

Among many honors bestowed upon Edwin Arlington Robinson, aside from the three Pulitzer Prizes for *Collected Poems*, *The Man Who Died Twice*, and *Tristram*, were Litt. D.'s from Yale in 1922 and Bowdoin College in 1925, membership in the National Institute of Arts and Letters and the National Academy of Arts and Letters, and a gold medal from the American Institute of Arts and Letters.

His books are: *The Torrent and the Night Before* (1896; privately printed), *The Children of the Night* (1897), *Captain Craig* (1902), *The Town Down the River* (1910), *The Man Against the Sky* (1916), *Merlin* (1917), *The Three Taverns* (1920), *Avon's Harvest* (1921), *Collected Poems* (1921, 1924, 1927), *Roman Bartholow* (1923), *The Man Who Died Twice* (1924), *Dionysus in Doubt* (1925), *Tristram* (1927), *Sonnets, 1889-1927* (1928), *Cavender's House* (1929), *Modred, A Fragment* (1929), *The Glory of the Nightingales* (1930), *Selected Poems* (edited by Bliss Perry; 1931), *Matthias at the Door* (1931), *Nicodemus* (1932), *Talifer* (1933), and *Amaranth* (1934).

Edwin Arlington Robinson says of poetry:

Poetry is a language that tells us, through a more or less emotional reaction, something that cannot be said. All poetry . . . does this. And it seems to me that poetry has two characteristics. One is that it is, after all, undefinable. The other is that it is eventually unmistakable.

Tributes to Robinson:

The present revival of poetry in America had its origin when Edwin Arlington Robinson published his first slender book containing *The Torrent and the Night Before,* a collection which a year later was merged in the better known title of *The Children of the Night.*

—JOHN GOULD FLETCHER

His poems do not invigorate, they mellow and subdue. But in our material day, the spirituality of Mr. Robinson's work is tonic and uplifting. . . .

He prunes every tendency to luxuriance from his style. He aims at the starkness of absolute truth, and granted that what he sees be the truth, he usually attains it.

This poetry is "cribbed, cabin'd and confined" to a remarkable degree, but it is undeniably, magnificently noble.

—AMY LOWELL

In one way his work is of the very greatest avail . . . it gives one a more thorough comprehension of human defeat. If it contains within itself no remedy, it leads at least to a better understanding of the disease which is forcing itself more and more gravely upon the attention of Americans.

—T. K. WHIPPLE

His tender verse, ironic and dramatic, shows much insight into human character. He is America's first poet.

—E. J. CLARK

Edwin Arlington Robinson is the poet of enigmatic character. He is, too, the poet of suspended drama. All his people are characters in a drama, of which the climax or the anticlimax has not been reached. Have they passed the worst, or do they face the worst? They do not know and we are not permitted to guess. Meanwhile, they show a defeated life— but yet a life that, knowing itself defeated, wins to a liberation which makes it a little free and a little triumphant. "We have each a darkening hill to climb," "I'll soon be changing as all do to something I have always been," "The lonely changelessness of dying": these are phrases that show Mr. Robinson's reading of life. He can write to a brave music,

[195]

but he uses traditional verse forms, often, I think, to mark a
mockery.

—Padraic Colum

Leonora Speyer (Born in Washington, D. C., in 1872)

Leonora von Stosch, an eighteen-year-old violinist
making her début with the Boston Symphony Orchestra,
little thought that thirty-one years later she would pub-
lish her first book of verse and five years after that she
would be awarded the Pulitzer Prize for her second
volume.

The young violinist had a mother of New England
stock, and her father was Count Ferdinand von Stosch,
a Prussian nobleman who became an American citizen
and fought for the Union in the Civil War. In those
early days she played with the New York Philharmonic
Orchestra and with other great orchestras. She married,
had four children, and lived abroad a good deal. Sir
Edgar Speyer, her second husband, whom she married
in 1902, was instrumental in bringing much modern
European music to England and published a German
translation of Keats's poems. His wife, however, did not
even begin to write until she was forty-four years old.
Since then she has published four volumes of verse and
won a number of prizes for her literary work. They make
an impressive list: The Blindman Prize, the Nation Prize,
the Poetry Society of America Prize, the Chicago Poetry
Award, and the Pulitzer Prize. She is the first woman
to have been honored by the presidency of the Poetry
Society of America, and she is a member of Phi Beta

[196]

Kappa. At present she lives in New York City and lectures widely on music and poetry.

Her books are: *Canopic Jar* (1921), *Fiddler's Farewell* (1926; awarded Pulitzer Prize for 1926), *Naked Heel* (1931), and *Slow Wall* (1939).

Tributes to Leonora Speyer:

What distinguishes the poetry of Leonora Speyer is its boldness. Amongst poems of today that are hesitating and tentative, hers are remarkable for a direct seizure of the subject and a swift presentation of the image.

—PADRAIC COLUM

Her poetic work gains in impact when presented as a whole; her contribution to the verse of our time defines itself in terms of a personality, an attitude toward life, a particular gift for word-music. . . . In her writing for the last twenty years Leonora Speyer has constantly given us occasion to remember that she was first of all a musician. . . . Mrs. Speyer's poems convey the impression of exactly the same personality that her violin playing once revealed—a very forceful, impassioned spirit; a capacity for deep feeling touched with glints of humor, an immense joy in the present moment.

—JOHN ERSKINE

She has attained a mastery of form, and particularly of rhythm. Her verse shows always unmistakably that it is the poetry of a woman who knows her own littleness, but is never lowly; and whose aspiration has such height and magnitude that it lifts her far beyond her conscious reach.

—L. G. MARSHALL

MARK VAN DOREN (Born near Hope, Illinois, in 1894)

Somewhere in his autobiography, *Three Worlds*, Carl Van Doren, the editor, author, and critic, refers to his brother Mark as "the most talented member of the Van Doren family"—a family in which ability was evidently general.

Born on an Illinois farm, the son of a country doctor, Mark Van Doren moved to Urbana at an early age, and won his A.B. and A.M. at the University of Illinois. His education was interrupted by the war, and he served two years in the Infantry. Then, after traveling in England and France on a Columbia fellowship, he took his Ph.D. from Columbia, where he is now Associate Professor of English and follows his quiet but productive career as a writer. His extracurricular activities have been his literary editorship of *The Nation* (1924-1928), his radio discussions of great books, his critical studies, anthologies, and books of poems.

Mr. Van Doren has been described as of medium height, with dark hair, strikingly dark eyes, tight lips, an attractive smile. "He is an interesting conversationalist with the ability to draw out his companion more than the latter realizes. His personality, sense of humor, and the saneness of his ideas make his college classes and lecture courses popular," says one writer. He is married to Dorothy Van Doren, the writer; has two sons, lives in New York City, and spends his leisure time on his Connecticut farm.

His books are: *Henry David Thoreau, A Critical Study* (1916), *The Poetry of John Dryden* (1920), *Spring Thunder and Other Poems* (1924), *American and British Literature Since 1890* (with Carl Van Doren, 1925; revised edition, 1939), *7 P.M. and Other Poems* (1926), *Edwin Arlington Robinson* (1927), *Now the Sky and Other Poems* (1928), *Jonathan Gentry* (1931), *Dick and Tom* (1931), *Dick and Tom in Town* (1932), *The Transients* (1935), *A Winter Diary and Other Poems* (1935), *The Last Look and Other Poems* (1937), *Studies in Metaphysical Poetry* (with Theodore Spencer, 1939), *Collected Poems* (1939), *Shakespeare* (1939), *Windless Cabins* (1940), *The Transparent Tree* (1940). He has edited *An American Bookshelf* (five volumes; 1927-1928), *An Anthology of World Poetry* (1928; revised edition, 1936), *An Autobiography of America* (1929), *The Roanoke Series of American Reprints* (two volumes; 1929), *American Poets, 1630-1930* (1932), *The Oxford Book of American Prose* (1932), and *An Anthology of English and American Poetry* (1936).

Mark Van Doren says of the poet:

The only conception of the poet is that he is a person who writes poetry.

Tributes to Mark Van Doren:

If not the most brilliant stylist of our times, one of the most accomplished craftsmen.

—ALLEN TATE

He seems while young to have become accustomed to the fact that his own particular world was already lost. And these things make him not altogether of our time. He is not solitary, but remote.

—JOHN PEALE BISHOP

There is a feeling of honesty of thought and craftsmanship in everything Mr. Van Doren writes. If he doesn't get excited about things he does try to extract the maximum of content from an experience. . . . He is an explorer into the quiet places of the mind and spirit.

—JOHN RITCHEY

The most significant major voice in American Poetry since Robert Frost.

—IRWIN EDMAN

AUDREY WURDEMANN (Born in Seattle, Washington, in 1911)

One American poet who won the Pulitzer Prize is a descendant of Shelley and Harriet Westbrook. Her name is Audrey Wurdemann.

This poet was educated at home, at the St. Nicholas School for Girls in Seattle, and at the University of Washington. She began to write when she was very young and in her early teens published some of her poems in the Bookfellow's *Stepladder* in Chicago. George Sterling, impressed by her talents, arranged for the publication of her first book of verse, *The House of Silk*, which was published before she entered the University. After college she traveled in the Orient and, in 1932, came to New York. Here she met the poet, Joseph Auslander, who was also a lecturer at Columbia and whom she married in 1933. In 1935 she won the Pulitzer Prize for her second book, *Bright Ambush*. She lives in New York.

Her books are: *The House of Silk* (1927), *Bright Ambush* (1934), *The Seven Sins* (1935), *Splendor in the Grass* (1936), and *Testament of Love* (1938).

Tributes to Audrey Wurdemann:

Miss Wurdemann is an honest artist, hoes her own row, and bides her time. She is the opposite of pretentious, and simply does what interests her, quite unimpressed by plaudits or lack of them. . . . She is a good craftsman.

Further experiences of life will enlarge her range, and she will have more original things to say, but already her verse shows evidence of rare texture. . . . Her poetry has a lyrical ease that can become treacherous.

—WILLIAM ROSE BENÉT

A great number of her lyrics have vividness, sincerity, charm and a technical precision that casts new shadows upon the familiarities of love, life, death.

—MARION STROEBEL

MARYA ZATURENSKA (Born in Kiev, Russia, 1902)

Here is the first Pulitzer Prize poet who was not born in America. For the first ten years of her life, Marya Zaturenska lived in a small Russian village. Then she was brought to America, and at fourteen she began to work in a factory. One day this young factory girl, who had only been to grammar school a few years, found Harriet Monroe's anthology, *The New Poetry*, on a public-library shelf. Here she discovered modern poetry, and soon she was writing it herself and seeing her own poems, which showed remarkable promise, in the magazine *Poetry*.

Her education continued at Valparaiso University, at the Library School of Wisconsin, and at the University of Wisconsin, where the Zona Gale Scholarship was awarded her for her literary talent. Other recognitions soon followed. She won *Poetry's* Memorial Prize for her "Elegies for John Reed." She won the Shelley Award, and the Guarantor's Prize was given her work after 1934, when her first book appeared. Then in 1938 came the Pulitzer Prize for her second volume, *Cold Morning Sky*. In 1925 she married Horace Gregory, the poet, lecturer, and critic. They have two children and live in New York City.

Her books are: *Threshold and Hearth* (1934), *Cold Morning Sky* (1937), and *The Listening Landscape* (1941).

Tributes to Marya Zaturenska:

Her poetry is distinctly of these times and yet occupied with a sense of timelessness. . . . Superficially these lyrics may seem to be pastoral-historical, but the synthesis is new, a combination of delicate observation and modern vision, of sharp personality and shadowed allegory.

—Louis Untermeyer

Her criterion of what to use has been "pure poetry." . . . She seeks the mellifluous line with restraint, and achieves her poetic release with striking success, conscious always of what she is doing, knowing it is dangerous and unfashionable and temporary. From the squawk of cities and the gnawing of the modern mind, she escapes to asylum and takes the veil.

—Marshall Schacht

Under the covers of her *Cold Morning Sky*, Marya Zaturenska has gathered a great landscape, a world which, though traditional, is peculiarly her own.

—D. Emerson